HOME LAND

REVEALED

HOME LAND
REVEALED ™

written by **MATT HURWITZ**

foreword by **ALEX GANSA**

FROM EXECUTIVE PRODUCERS ALEX GANSA AND HOWARD GORDON

CHRONICLE BOOKS
SAN FRANCISCO

Contents

FOREWORD by Alex Gansa

I am a writer. My title says Executive Producer, but I am, at the end of the day, a writer. And there is no greater feeling for a writer of television than to deliver fifty or so pages every few weeks to an extraordinarily talented group of actors and filmmakers and to watch them transform those pages into an episode better than he could have ever imagined. Such has been my privilege for three seasons on *Homeland*.

Every successful television show is a miracle. So many forces conspire against its survival from the very start, and so many hard choices must be made—narrative choices, casting choices, staffing choices, programming choices—any one of which can prove fatal. I know that people don't like to hear success explained away as luck, but in the case of *Homeland*'s debut, there is simply no other explanation. Everything that could go right did, and everything that usually goes wrong didn't.

I am often asked: Why do you think the series is so popular, what makes it work? I often say: I wish I knew. But in my heart, I know the answer. Claire Danes and Damian Lewis. They are the twin suns at the center of the *Homeland* galaxy, and, at the risk of exhausting the metaphor, it was the gravitational force between them that compelled our fans to invest so deeply in the story from the very beginning.

Since that first season, many gifted people have joined the *Homeland* team— Lesli Linka Glatter, Dave Klein, Patrick Harbinson, Rupert Friend, F. Murray Abraham, Tracy Letts, Nazanin Boniadi, Zuleikha Robinson, Shaun Toub among them. But the framers of the initial twelve episodes deserve special mention here, for they built the show from the ground up.

Of all the people who put a significant imprimatur on *Homeland*, Michael Cuesta has received the least public recognition. And I'd like to set the record straight here. Of his many great directorial gifts, perhaps Michael's greatest is his ability to design scenes that convey the impression that real life is happening. He made watching *Homeland* an intensely voyeuristic experience. If not for his incredible eye and impeccable taste, the series would have been a far lesser enterprise.

Superstitious, I read every first draft of every *Homeland* script in the same chair, taking notes with the same pen, starting at exactly the same time: 5:30 A.M. And, of all the drafts I've read, I will forever remember four. Alex Cary's "Grace," Chip Johannessen's "Clean Skin," Henry Bromell's "The Good Soldier," and Meredith Stiehm's "The Weekend." Not because they were necessarily each writer's best work on the show, but because they were each writer's first work on the show. And because, by the time I had turned the last page of each script, I knew that I had hired a major talent. They have been called brilliant, they have been called a murderers' row, they are the finest group of writers I have ever sat in a story room with. My debt—and *Homeland*'s debt—to them cannot be overstated.

Michael Klick's producing work on *Homeland* has been nothing short of Herculean. He created a studio in Charlotte out of nothing, put together our crew there, and has bravely led them for three years. I may be the showrunner, but he runs the show.

Our supporting cast was also stellar, especially Mandy Patinkin, Morena Baccarin, and Morgan Saylor. Farther down the call sheet: David Harewood,

Navid Negahban, David Marciano, James Rebhorn, Amy Hargreaves, Jackson Pace, Diego Klattenhoff, Sarita Choudhury, and Jamey Sheridan all took vastly underwritten roles and fleshed them out in front of the camera with professionalism and panache.

Praise must also be heaped upon our two Directors of Photography (Chris Manley and Nelson Cragg), our two Production Designers (Patti Podesta and John Kretschmer), our two Costume Designers (Marina Draghici and Katina Le Kerr), and our five Casting Directors (Junie Lowry-Johnson, Libby Goldstein, Judy Henderson, and Craig and Lisa Mae Fincannon).

Few things are more humbling for a writer than to watch how music can elevate an ordinary scene into something transcendent. Sean Callery's brittle and beautiful score accomplishes this magic every week. His main title theme is, in my opinion, a work of genius.

Katie O'Hara, our co-producer in charge of post production, rarely sleeps during the season, and her handpicked trio of editors (Jordan Goldman, Joe Hobeck, and Terry Kelley) consistently deliver cuts of breathtaking clarity and artistry. It is in their editing bays and on the dub stage—with our brilliant sound mixers Nello Torri, Alan Decker, and Craig Dellinger—where the final draft of each episode is written.

My wife Lauren is my secret weapon. She notes every draft and every cut of every episode, and the long hours we've logged together talking story over the dinner table and on walks in the hills behind our house have shaped the series in important and immeasurable ways.

Homeland would not exist without the Israeli hit show Hatufim and its creator Gideon Raff, nor without WME agent Rick Rosen who was the first person to see potential in the material as an American series.

Twentieth Television Co-Chairmen Dana Walden and Gary Newman and Fox 21 President Bert Salke are our most ardent fans and partners. The level of studio support they provide this show is unprecedented in my experience in the entertainment business.

Finally, however, the decision to put *Homeland* on the air came down to one man. David Nevins. Newly minted as President of Showtime, he gambled and chose this project as his first. Major thanks to him and to his super-talented lieutenants Gary Levine and Randy Runkle, who give real meaning to the title Creative Executive.

It is only fitting to give Howard Gordon the last bow. He brought me onto *Homeland*. He and I wrote the pilot together. And afterwards, knowing that all ships steer more truly with one captain, he graciously excused himself from the bridge. The most generous-spirited person I know, my dear friend of more than thirty years, Howard is the man I try to emulate every day as a showrunner and as a human being. A sign above his desk reads: Work Hard. Be Nice To People. Indeed.

—Alex Gansa
  Celestino, Mexico
  March 8, 2014

OPPOSITE: *Homeland* creators Howard Gordon (center) and Alex Gansa (right) visit with *Homeland Revealed* author Matt Hurwitz in Gordon's office on the Fox lot.

RIGHT: Executive producer/writer Alex Gansa discusses a scene with Damian Lewis on the front lawn of the Brody house location for Season 1's "Marine One."

CREATING HOMELAND

★ AFTER RUNNING ONE OF THE

most successful thrill rides in TV history for eight years, where does one go next?

Executive producers/writers Howard Gordon and Alex Gansa were beginning to see the light at the end of the tunnel on Fox's mega-hit 24. The show's eighth and last season was in production when Gordon received a call in late December 2009 from his agent, Rick Rosen, who was on his way home from Israel. "He said, 'I have your next show,'" the producer recalls.

That next show was Israeli filmmaker Gideon Raff's *Hatufim* (or *Prisoners of War*), created for Israel's Keshet Broadcasting. Raff had begun the show with a three-page synopsis, after which he was given the go-ahead from network executive Avi Nir to write a full season's scripts. Impressed by the results, Nir asked Raff to translate the first episode into English and gave the English translation to Rosen, before even a frame of footage had been shot.

Upon receiving the script from Rosen, Gordon and Gansa were immediately impressed and wanted to see more. "America had been engaged in two conflicts for ten years, but there was no strong character on American television that really reflected the price of war," Gordon recalls. Adds Gansa, "One of the things I loved about what Gideon did was how well he rendered the dramatic implications of coming home after being away for such a long time. There were a lot of soldiers coming home to America from Iraq and Afghanistan. That reentry and reintegration back into their former lives was really interesting to us." There was also a thriller element, Raff notes. "There is a lot of suspense in the unpredictability of someone coming back after being missing for years. There's a secret behind their eyes."

Gordon and Gansa met with Raff at the Luxe Hotel on Sunset Boulevard in Los Angeles to talk about how to adapt the series for American audiences. "We started with conversations about what we thought would work for an American audience and what was more Israeli," Raff recalls. Israelis, for example, negotiate for the return of soldiers and Americans do not. *Hatufim* features two characters, Uri and Nimrod, who are released after years of negotiation, not released in a military operation, as Brody would be. "Howard and Alex talked about the zeitgeist in America. Both shows are very successful in honing in on those nerves in our respective societies."

Gordon and Gansa realized that creating their series would require a wholesale reinvention of Raff's series. While some of Raff's original elements would show up in *Homeland*—such as the returnee curling up on his floor for comfort, punching a reporter, secretive finger taps, sexual dysfunction, or the wife recoiling at the sight of her husband's scars—they began to think of how to make a show that would work in the States.

Raff returned to Israel to begin production of *Hatufim*'s first season, but he stayed in regular contact with his American friends, whose gears had begun to turn. "Howard and I have a Socratic method," says Gansa. "We get out and walk, especially at the beginning of projects. Those are the most exciting, but also the most excruciating days."

It was on one such walk that it was decided to combine the two returnees into one—Brody. "We said, 'There's too much real estate with two guys—we can't service it,'" Gordon remembers. "Frankly, Brody was hard enough to define. That character became more special when he became one character."

Brody retained key elements of both of Raff's characters, Uri and Nimrod, as well as of Amiel, the third prisoner whom Nimrod believes he was forced to kill (as Brody believes about Tom Walker). The result: a damaged man with a secret, a skilled liar from whom the truth may never be known.

While *Hatufim* focuses mainly on the family dramas of the two returnees, Gordon and Gansa knew that American audiences loved the thrill ride of suspense. Raff notes, "It was very clear to me that the family drama, the deep exploration of post-traumatic stress disorder and the wound in Israeli society, is less relevant to American audiences than the actual investigation—what is the secret that they're hiding?"

"In *Hatufim*," Gordon adds, "there wasn't actually a real-time threat. It's never quite clear if one of those guys has been turned." And prisoner exchanges in Israel are the subject of great debate. "We didn't feel an American prisoner of war coming back to Alexandria, Virginia, would have that same currency," Gansa says. "That's why we gave him this ulterior motive," revenge for the death of Nazir's son, Issa.

And what about the heroine? Having just come off 24, Gansa notes, "We asked ourselves, how were we going to differentiate this character from Jack Bauer? If you look at Carrie, you'll see that a lot of choices were made in reaction to Jack. Carrie doesn't carry a gun; she isn't an action hero. And she lives in her brain, not in her physicality." She is also unstable, but the audience still roots for her.

Unlike *Hatufim*'s Iris, who is assigned to connect with Uri to find out what he is hiding, Carrie is self-motivated. She has her own beliefs about Abu Nazir and a turned soldier that drive her, beliefs she spends the entire first season trying to prove. "That was actually the thing that got Alex and me excited to begin with—the idea of having somebody who had a theory no one else believed," says Gordon.

Brody's wife, Jessica, is actually an amalgamation of *Hatufim*'s two wives: Talia, the faithful spouse who waited and campaigned for seventeen years for her husband, Nimrod's, return, and Nurit, who, after such a length of time, assumed Uri was dead and married his brother, a decision that she is derided for upon Uri's surprise return. In *Homeland*, Jessica waited but, while she did, fell in love with Brody's best friend, Mike Faber. Says Raff, "In Israel, we grow up thinking about, 'Would I wait? Would I want my spouse to wait or not?' It's less relevant in America. But it takes a toll on both types of women. So they tried to combine the two conflicts into one character."

Upon the premiere of *Hatufim* in March 2010 to great acclaim (it would eventually win the Israeli equivalent of an Emmy), Gordon traveled to Israel to announce the adaptation of the series in America. In mid-September, after *Homeland*'s pilot script had been written, Showtime executive David Nevins picked up the series, and planning for production of the pilot began. "We were on our way," says Gordon.

WHAT IS PRISONERS OF WAR?

■ Every fan of *Homeland* sees the title each week, "Based on the original Israeli series *Prisoners of War* by Gideon Raff." But what is *Prisoners of War*?

Prisoners of War (or *Hatufim*, in Hebrew) depicts the experience of POW returnees and their families.

The series focuses on three Israeli soldiers taken prisoner 17 years prior: Nimrod Klein (portrayed by Yoram Toledano), a seemingly strong, balanced soldier, and Uri Zach (Ishai Golan), his fellow prisoner, clearly damaged from the experience. The two have an immensely strong bond after years of captivity together.

Following years of negotiations, the two are finally released from captivity. Before returning to their homes, they spend a period of time at a "rehabilitation facility," under the direction of a military psychologist, Major Haim Cohen (Gal Zaid). Cohen attempts to determine if the two are hiding anything.

Cohen enlists a pretty female agent, Iris (Sendi Bar), to attempt to start a romance with Uri, to find out what he and Nimrod know. Cohen uncovers a torturous, shame-filled experience the two men are hiding in which Nimrod beat a third prisoner, Amiel Ben-Horin (popular Israeli star Assi Cohen) to death. Cohen determines that they were only meant to believe that Amiel was dead and that he is, in fact, still alive and part of the terrorist group that captured him.

When the two soldiers are finally released to their families, Nimrod returns to a strong wife, Talia (Yael Abecassis) and their two children. Talia suffers through attempts to reconnect with her husband, both physically and emotionally, while their kids, daughter Dana and son Hatzav, struggle to have any relationship with the father they don't know.

Uri returns to find that his wife Nurit (Mili Avital) has moved on, marrying his brother and raising a son. Nurit struggles with whether to give up her family commitment to rejoin with Uri.

As the series portrays, those held against their will are not the only ones whose lives are thrown into disarray. Raff notes, "On a certain level, the community is a prisoner of war; maybe the whole country. We're all prisoners of war."

Hatufim captives Amiel Ben-Horin (Assi Cohen), Uri Zach (Ishai Golan) and Nimrod Klein (Yoram Toledano).

MEET THE CHARACTERS

CARRIE MATHISON

CIA AGENT CARRIE MATHISON WANTS only one thing: to prevent terror against American citizens. But her complex, driven personality can make her appear as an incredible asset to some and a risky liability to others. She is *driven*, whether she likes it or not—and she not only likes it, she lives for it.

Carrie didn't start out quite as colorful as we know her today. In fact, she didn't start out as "Carrie." At the time they were writing the pilot, Gordon and Gansa had just seen Danes's Emmy-winning performance in *Temple Grandin*. "We were very specific in our minds that the character was of a certain age, with a certain energy and intelligence and vulnerability," Gordon recalls. "We created a character who was very much like Claire Danes—in fact, we called the character Claire."

Gordon and Gansa sent the script to the actor, who, by good fortune, was available and liked what she saw. "She was incredibly capable, smart, and had a lot of authority, but also this really interesting vulnerability," Danes says. "It's always interesting to play somebody who has a secret. But here was a secret agent who had another secret buried beneath all of that."

Interestingly, that secret—Carrie's mental illness—was not originally part of her character. After the pilot had been picked up by Showtime, Gordon and Gansa were called in for a meeting. "They were tremendously excited about what we'd done," Gansa recalls, "but there was a sense that Carrie was not a cable-worthy character yet. She was always a pariah. She always had an unpopular view. But there was nothing that anchored it." The network had successful shows about a drug addict, a multiple personality, and a serial killer. "There were all these bigger-than-life pathologies. They wanted something to make her richer or deeper."

On suggestion from Gansa's wife, the concept of a bipolar disorder was added. "We had gone through every possible pathology. But being bipolar excused her unbalanced and erratic behavior, in a strange way, because she had a condition that she was fighting. And there was an aspirational quality to her actually overcoming it at some point." Danes, who came onboard after that decision, also liked the way the writers made use of it. "I never wanted her condition to become a gimmick. And nobody on the show ever made it 'cheap,' which is why it's so special."

Both the writing team and Danes did research on bipolar disorder, utilizing Kay Redfield Jamison's book *An Unquiet Mind* as a key resource (as was Jamison herself). In addition, writer Meredith Stiehm also happens to have a sister who suffers from the illness. "Meredith was often the voice of Carrie, particularly with regard to bipolar disorder," Danes notes. "She knows how the illness works, so that was a serendipitous gift for us to have her onboard."

Danes herself also spoke with another author, Julie A. Fast, interviewed friends who knew of the psychology of the disease, and studied YouTube videos to get a sense of the unique physical behavior bipolar patients have. "Carrie is what's known as bipolar 1," the actor explains. "They tend to be more manic than depressive and have a more rapid cycle than bipolar 2 people." Mania is also a bit more interesting, for storytelling purposes, than the depressive side. "They have a hard time with personal boundaries when they're manic, and they're very charismatic. They're attractive and attracting. And they are often very promiscuous. They self-medicate with alcohol, tend not to sleep, and talk at a faster clip. And they're very imposing. There's a point on the continuum when they are high-performing, in fact outperforming everyone around them, something they always strive for and try to maintain."

Patients like Carrie, when they can, will tend to reject the medications that are there to help prevent the up-down swings of the disease, writer Chip Johannessen notes. "It tones them down. They feel it takes life that was Technicolor and makes it black and white." His colleague, Alex Cary, likens Carrie's behavior in such instances to that of a German shepherd he once owned. "I had a house with one of those invisible electric fences and a collar for the dog. I would see her go through it and grit her teeth; I would see the determination and courage just to break free. I've always thought of Carrie that way."

Carrie is also a fan of jazz, again, something not originally considered when her character was created. "It's very improvisational and symbolic of her inner life," says director Michael Cuesta, who first brought up Carrie's affinity to the genre. "It's complex and unpredictable, just like Carrie."

Its place in her work first appears in the pilot, when Carrie, having picked up a man in a bar, has a sudden realization about Brody's apparent signaling to his handlers via finger tapping signals. Production designer Patti Podesta first came up with the idea, she recalls. "Cuesta and I were talking, and he said, 'How would she figure that out from looking at the jazz band?' I said, 'She'd be watching the fingering of the musicians, and it would make sense to her, because that's how her brain works,' and everyone went, 'Yeah!'"

Her drive to pursue terrorism—and Abu Nazir in particular—is considered to stem from an experience in Iraq, where she served as as a case officer. "I think she came of age there, really," Danes notes.

The writers surmise that she was, at one point, close with a guide/translator, whom Carrie saw killed. "They had been separated in a crowd, in a flash mob in the streets of Baghdad," says Cary. "He had been taken as a traitor and strung up on a bridge and burned alive, and she had been in the crowd, unable to do anything about it, and watched. For me, that's what has driven her to fight terrorism."

Carrie remains a loner, much like her mentor, Saul Berenson, and other great members of the agency. "She's a little bit like Edward Scissorhands," Danes says. "She's afraid of getting close to people, because she knows the kind of damage her condition can wreak." Her relationship is truly with her job. "The best way she knows to take care of herself is to work," says Cary. "When she's working, she's really on top."

Despite her very human flaws, Carrie's heart and underlying drive come from the right place. "She is a true patriot," says Danes. "She makes huge personal sacrifices in order to do her work well. And we admire her for that—it kind of justifies all of her less charming qualities."

WHAT IS BIPOLAR DISORDER?

Some of the most fascinating parts of Carrie's personality come from the fact that she suffers from bipolar disorder, formerly called manic depression. People who are bipolar experience distinct—and severe—mood swings. "It's not somebody who just feels lousy in the afternoon or gets irritated in the evening," explains Carolinas HealthCare neuropsychiatrist Dr. Jay Yeomans, a consultant to *Homeland*. "These are distinct mood changes, not precipitated by any event, and last for days or months."

Untreated, bipolar individuals experience both severe depression followed by bouts of manic activity. The depression is much worse than for people who suffer from more common "unipolar" depression, Yeomans says. "They have to pull themselves out of bed, drag themselves around the house all day, and experience inappropriate guilt and remorse." They often experience disturbances in sleep, appetite, and sex drive, have a lack of interest, and are "anergic," meaning they have absolutely no energy.

The flip side is their manic behavior, characterized by unbridled energy. "They generally will multitask, doing two or three things at once, and tell you they 'feel great.' And they're not insomniacs. They don't have trouble sleeping; they don't want to sleep. They have no reason to."

There is also a sense of grandiosity with bipolars, a feeling of being unstoppable and having a "special mission," which, in Carrie's case, is actually true. "There's a feeling of 'nothing is going to stop me from achieving my goal,' an obsessive quality, a determination. Even though people tell Carrie to just drop it and move on, she won't let go."

Bipolar people will engage in incredibly risky behavior. "There's a hypersexuality, but other kinds of things too, like getting into accidents, trespassing. They're very outspoken, because, for them, there are no boundaries. They'll say things in public that are just outrageous."

Carrie, he notes, is "mixed bipolar," which means she has plenty of energy but then becomes dysphoric. "Classically, the person who is manic is really gregarious. They can actually be very entertaining. But a mixed bipolar can have all that energy but be really irritable and dysphoric."

Bipolar disorder can be treated with several different drugs. On *Homeland*, Carrie is treated with lithium, a safe, naturally occurring salt that acts as a mood stabilizer, to level out the peaks and troughs of the patient's mood swings. "It's not used as much today as some other drugs, but it's still quite effective." Clozapine, which Virgil finds Carrie taking in the pilot, is more typically prescribed for schizophrenics, rarely for those who are bipolar. "It's one of the 'big guns,'" Yeomans says. If they don't respond to medications, patients may opt for electroconvulsive therapy (ECT), as Carrie does at the end of Season 1.

Yeomans was impressed with Dane's performance. "She did her homework. It is uncanny how well she portrays somebody with bipolar disorder."

NICHOLAS BRODY

NICHOLAS BRODY IS AN UNUSUAL CHAR-
acter in television. Audiences traditionally
would never root for a terrorist, but never has
been both as loved and reviled as Brody has. He's
both a victim and a perpetrator, a man with a
family we love, but with another relationship
we hope will survive as well. He's incredibly
complex to watch: you never know which Brody
you're going to get.

"Because of the narrative experiment of not
knowing whether he was or wasn't a terrorist,
there were multiple points of view," producer
Howard Gordon explains. "There was Brody
viewed through the public frame of television
as a hero, through the private frame of Carrie's
surveillance, and through his own remembered
past as a prisoner of war. He was a bit of a cipher."

Finding an actor who could deal with all
these aspects of the character proved difficult.
At first the producers searched without any luck.
But director Michael Cuesta was a fan of fellow
indie director Lodge Kerrigan (who would later
direct Season 2's "State of Independence"), and
had seen his 2004 film, *Keane*, which starred

Damian Lewis. "It's one man's odyssey through
the underbelly of New York searching for his
daughter," Lewis describes. "We begin to question his sanity and wonder whether the daughter
actually ever existed."

In late December 2010, Cuesta got the film
in front of producer Alex Gansa and suggested
Lewis for the role of Brody. "I think they needed
to see an actor who could explore the darker
areas of the mind," Lewis says. Gansa had
intended to watch only ten minutes of the film,
but found himself hooked by Lewis's performance. Says Gordon, "He called me the next
day and said, 'You gotta see this.'"

Lewis had a few concerns that he wanted to
be clear about before jumping in. "Early on, I
told them I wouldn't feel comfortable playing
an upstanding American Marine who became
violent just because he had converted to Islam. I
thought that would be untrue and irresponsible,
and I just didn't want to tell that story. If they
could find a way for the benevolent aspects of
the Islamic faith to be there to nurture him, to
be a sustaining force of good in his life, then I'd
be interested." Gordon and Gansa assured the
actor that was their intention, and, two days
before Christmas, Lewis was offered the role.

One thing that was not an issue for the producers was the fact that Lewis is British, and, naturally, speaks with a British accent when not in character. Gansa says of his star's American accent as Brody, "It doesn't come from anywhere—it's not mid-Atlantic, not southern. It's actually unrecognizable as a real American accent—except that it's perfect."

Brody is complex because he has formed many layers of personality in order to survive. Says writer Alex Cary, "What makes Brody a really fascinating character is that he's not a fully developed person. There's something a little stunted about him. This is a guy who was thrown into a hole for eight years, and been deeply, deeply abused. And he's a guy who's chosen to be a blunt instrument, to a certain extent."

Brody is constantly at odds with himself as he tries to keep all of the plates spinning. At any given moment, though, that's difficult to see, thanks to Lewis's skillful portrayal. "Brody has all these conflicting layers going on inside himself," he notes. "He's somehow able to compartmentalize them—to push aside 'I'm gonna kill the Vice President' for the few minutes while he has dinner with his family."

Conveying that in a believable manner, Lewis says, requires him to make the same kind of shift Brody makes. "Trying to play too many things in one moment is an error," the actor explains. "I make definitive decisions and play one thing at a time. Brody loves his family, and he's trying to make that evening meal work, so I just decide to play that, and I play it to the hilt. You may have seen Brody lying to his family in the previous episode, but, as an actor, you just have to trust that the work is done for you, in the audience's eyes. They know they've seen Brody lie, they know he's hiding from his family, that he's now a Muslim and in contact with a terrorist. I don't play those things at the dinner table at the same time. I just play the dinner table."

Brody easily shifts from one life to the next—he's a chameleon. "Damian will choose moments to show this other side of Brody," says writer Chip Johannessen.

Adds Cary, "In one scene, you can see him play the victim and the terrorist, one after the other. That's Damian's gift, doing that without words. You can see the switch turn."

Claire Danes and Damian Lewis take a break during filming of Veterans Support Group scene in Season 1's "Semper I."

Notes Lewis, "He's constantly active, he's transitive, he moves forward. And that makes him compelling to watch."

Brody is, of course, the world's greatest liar. "You're so used to the idea that he lies about everything, you never believe him," says Johannessen. There are often so many untruths happening at once, it's hard to keep track. "His whole existence is a lie," says writer Meredith Stiehm. "Every step he takes, he's got to check himself."

That ability to lie, says Gideon Raff, stems from Brody's years in captivity, something the producer discovered researching *Hatufim*. "Prisoners wouldn't call it 'lying,'" he states. "They would call it 'surviving.' They learn to

lie to survive. Lying about how you feel, and how broken you really are, is a little bit of a victory in captivity. And it can continue even after a prisoner is freed," as in Brody's case to an incredible degree. "Even if a prisoner told the truth, no one would believe him."

And then there's the question, in Season 1, is Brody a terrorist or isn't he? Initially, the producers didn't tell Lewis the answer to that question, only that there would be some ambiguity in the character. "That's what's interesting about him," says Cary. "He's somebody who's trying to figure out who he is, as much as we're trying to figure it out. And we figure it out at about the same time he does, when he flips that switch."

SAUL BERENSON

A WARM-HEARTED, COMMITTED, PRIN-cipled man. If you think that sounds like Saul Berenson, you've hit the nail on the head.

Like Carrie, Saul is an outsider, even within the CIA. "We started with the durable trope of the righteous insider-outsider," says Michael Cuesta, even to the point of making Saul Jewish, likely one of the few Jews inside the agency.

Saul isn't one of the younger, politically motivated CIA members like David Estes. "He's not part of the old boys' club," explains show-runner Alex Gansa. "That's why we gave him a beard." Mandy Patinkin's casting in the part was actually contingent upon him growing one. Saul rolls up his sleeves much like a college professor. "Everybody around Saul takes more care with their appearance. And he rarely wears a tie."

Gansa had been a fan of Patinkin's since seeing him on Broadway in 1982 in *Sunday in the Park with George*, in which the actor, most unusually, wore a beard. "I've never been able to get that out of my head. Whenever I see Mandy without a beard, that's not Mandy. It makes him more accessible, more paternal."

It's Saul's paternal qualities that, in many ways, bond him to Carrie. "He's really her dad, as far as the construction of a TV drama goes," explains writer Alex Cary. "He wants her to be successful." The two fill many different roles with each other, actor Claire Danes informs. "They're best friends, they're peers. They're mentor and mentee. And he's kind of avuncular. She has enormous respect for him—his opinion carries a lot of weight for her. She does not trust easily, and she trusts him very deeply. And if that trust is ever compromised, it's very painful for her."

When Carrie occasionally crosses her mentor, it is very hurtful for Saul as well, but he is always ready to forgive. "He's a deeply compassionate guy," says producer Howard Gordon. "If he feels for Carrie, we feel for Carrie. And if Carrie betrays him, we feel that betrayal. He gives her an audience and indulges her cautiously."

Saul is one of the few people who can see through Carrie's mania, to see beyond what, to anyone else, is simply a crazy person. "He tolerates her erratic behavior, because he knows there's an end product that is brilliant," Gansa says. "She gets there in ways that are unconventional, and he's willing to sit through all of the erratic stuff to get to the gold."

It's that willingness to see something beyond that makes Saul tick for the audience. "Unlike Estes, he's willing to think outside the box," director Michael Cuesta says. "With Carrie, you have to, because she exists out of the box. And Saul knows that if everyone's thinking the basic thinking, whose brain works like no other brain? Carrie's. It's like the savant brain. And he knows she's like the brilliant tiger that's in the cage, who, every once in a while, gets out. So he's got to be her minder, in that respect."

Patinkin's genuine, natural portrayal is no accident. His years of careful stagecraft are evident, even in ways the viewer doesn't consciously notice, writer Chip Johannessen notes. "Mandy blocks things so that he has places to move and things to do, things that feed the scene and give it real life. He can make a sandwich, and it's riveting," such as in Season 1's "Representative Brody," where a lonely Saul, working late, uses a ruler from his desk to make "dinner" out of peanut butter and crackers.

"We think of Saul as a talker, but when his wife is about to leave in a taxi, instead of talking, he's taking the suitcases back out of the cab and putting them down on the ground. Mandy puts things in that are so perfect that you don't

notice them. He takes this slightly professorial guy and infuses him, very subtly, so that you don't see it, with this huge amount of energy. When you see him work on set, you can't believe anything can be that good."

JESSICA BRODY

IN THE INITIAL SHOOT OF THE PILOT, Jessica was played by petite Scottish-born actress Laura Fraser (see "The Pilot," page 46). But the part was re-cast once the series was picked up. By the end of May 2010, they had arrived at Morena Baccarin's front door. The actor had just wrapped the starring role in ABC's *V*, and, she recalls, "Within that week I went in for *Homeland* and got it, and two weeks later, I shipped off to Charlotte."

Most appealing to Baccarin was the incredible spot Jessica was in. "She's in this impossible, heartbreaking situation, where she thinks she's lost the person she loves. She's allowed herself to suffer through that loss, and after holding out hope that he's coming back, has finally put that to rest and allowed herself to love—and then has that pulled out from under her. I thought that plight was incredibly complex. And I liked the way she handled it, with strength and, at the same time, vulnerability. It allows for Brody to be the victim, because she doesn't play the victim."

Baccarin was careful to avoid reviewing Laura Fraser's depiction of Jessica in the original pilot. "I started fresh. I didn't really watch Laura's work, because I didn't want it to influence any instincts that I had about the character."

While Fraser had a sweet, delicate beauty about her, Baccarin brought a sexual confidence that served the show in a different way. Notes writer Alex Cary, "You can't deny Morena's physical beauty. Do Marines really have wives that hot? The fact is, yeah, they do."

One thing she brought with her from *V* was her character's iconic pixie haircut—revealed in *Homeland*'s fifth episode, shot nearly two months later, when Jessica comes home with a "new" haircut. "They originally thought that hairstyle was too hip and cosmopolitan for a woman living in suburban Virginia married to a Marine," she says. So a custom wig and hair extensions were hand-carried from Los Angeles and used in the first four episodes, until everyone agreed it was time to abandon them. "I asked many times, 'Can we get rid of this thing?' Eventually they realized it didn't look that great."

With only a week or so to prep, Baccarin went online to research what military wives experience. "I visited chat rooms, support groups for army wives," she explains. "I was really struck by how brave these women were. I think the men couldn't leave home if they didn't know that they had a strong partner to take care of things. Their wives are a huge support system for the men. They keep things the same in the house while they're away, so they don't feel that they've missed out on anything," much the way Jessica has done.

Jessica is just as strong as Baccarin's real-life models. "I think of a fierce lioness, in a sense," Baccarin says, "Jessica's not aggressive, but her priority is protecting her family. She's not a stupid woman, but she's simple. The things she has in life are enough for her."

Director Michael Cuesta agrees. "Jessica operates in the real world. She's simple and uncomplicated, and the way Morena plays that, it makes her a very real character, someone people can really relate to."

Instead of playing up her glamour, Baccarin makes Jessica a real mom, even down to blasting an angry "Dammit!" after discovering an overcooked dinner in the oven. "I feel very comfortable in the Brody house set, and I always try to find 'business' to do, whether it's folding something or cleaning something. If you're the mother of two kids, you're very rarely just sitting around."

Jessica doesn't operate well in a world of unpredictability, the world that Brody brings home with him. Says Cary, "She doesn't fully understand what Brody's been through. Jessica has to face the fact that what he's been through is probably so awful that he may not want to talk about it. So there's a distance from his problems—a tentativeness, that's aloof and cold sometimes, but tender at the same time—until it really gets out of control, and then, obviously, she responds. It's a very difficult role to play, and Morena is extraordinary dealing with all that."

DANA BRODY

IF THERE'S ONE THING DANA BRODY can do, it's deliver the truth. Whether it's to her mother, her father, her mom's boyfriend, her own boyfriend, or even the Vice President. She tells it like it is.

"She's intelligent, and she's very intuitive about things," says producer Alex Gansa. "And she's not the typical teenager," something that made Dana attractive to actor Morgan Saylor when she learned about the role at her home in Atlanta at age fifteen.

"I think the word they used to describe her in the synopsis for the audition was 'dry,'" Saylor recalls. "So I took that as not an annoying teenager, not a brat. I wanted her to be someone that felt understandable to the audience, someone that adults wouldn't just brush off."

About the casting process, Gansa remembers, "We had seen a procession of young actresses—the usual eye-rolling, gum-chewing, spring breakers, older than their years." Then Saylor walked in. "She kicked off her shoes when she came into the casting room and curled up on the couch like a little cat." The young actor knew how to create the Dana vibe that Gansa and director Michael Cuesta were looking for. "I just sat on the leather couch and tried to seem like I didn't give a fuck," she says. "That's Dana."

Saylor also brought a delivery that was unlike any of the other girls who read, something that has stayed with the character. "She brought her own cadence to the scenes that made the words feel real and utterly captivating," says Gansa, describing the unique pauses the actor introduces into lines, as Dana reaches for a poignant thought. "She can take the text and always make it fresh," agrees Cuesta. "She just owns it, and I never know what she's going to do. And it's always right."

Dana has a "bullshit meter" that never stops working. "I think she's brave and just doesn't give a shit what people think," the actor explains. "She's often searching for the right words, just right beliefs, because she doesn't take any BS." Dana will go out on a limb to call anyone's bluff or to make things right. "It's unique to have a teenager be the one to be the truest, especially among the adults, something I really like that they did with her."

That quality comes in handy, particularly with regard to her relationship with both of her parents, Morena Baccarin notes. "The writers use that quality in Dana in such a great way," the actor says. "Because kids know how to push their parents' buttons, and she knows how to push mine, certainly. But it's also the voice of truth. It's what people are thinking. Most of the time what Dana is saying is, basically, 'Does anybody see that this is fucked up?' Jessica has to keep it together, so she can't allow herself to process how fucked up the situation is. But Dana can. And for the audience, it's great to have a character to see through all that."

The writers quickly spotted Saylor's talent and began writing more for her to take advantage of it, notes Chip Johannessen. "I had written a scene for her in the first season's "Clean Skin,"

where she and Brody go for a walk and talk by a fence. She proved she could deliver, so we gave her more and more to do," eventually culminating in having it be Dana who talks Brody down from setting off a bomb at the end of Season 1.

It's evident at the beginning of the third season that the experiences Dana has suffered through with her father have taken their toll on the character, though they've remained interesting to Saylor throughout. "I've been with Dana during the most pivotal time in her life, after Brody comes back," she says. "It's been interesting to go along with her on that roller coaster. I feel like I've been there since the beginning. She's an amazing girl."

> "*Most of the time what Dana is saying is, basically, 'Does anybody see that this is fucked up? Jessica has to keep it together, so she can't allow herself to process how fucked up the situation is.'*"
>
> — MORENA BACCARIN, JESSICA BRODY

DAVID ESTES

CIA DEPUTY DIRECTOR DAVID ESTES IS a climber, who sees himself one day running the agency, a goal that doesn't include an agent with a mental pathology who regularly goes off book.

As far as Carrie Mathison is concerned, David Estes is the "party of no." If Saul suggests a task for her, the CIA assistant director is pretty much not interested. "And with good reason," says director Michael Cuesta. "She could screw things up. She's a wild card, and David Estes lives in a world of absolutes."

"He's a linear thinker," explains the British actor David Harewood, who portrayed him. "He's very much a company man who likely has been overpromoted. He hasn't got Saul's experience—he's never been in the field. And he hasn't got the ability to think laterally, to think on his feet."

Writer Chip Johannessen agrees. "He's very political. He's not flatly incompetent, but his skills have more to do with *getting* the job than with *doing* the job. In that sense, he's over his head."

Estes sees himself as part of the new generation of CIA, at one point telling Saul, "The world has changed, Saul, right under your fucking nose," Harewood points out. "He's telling him, 'You guys are dinosaurs. We're this younger generation, who are computer literate and can kill 60,000 people by remote-controlled drones without having to understand the effect it has on the people on the ground.' We just push a button, and 'Let's go.'"

It's not until Season 1's "Marine One" that we realize Estes has been involved in a cover-up, along with Vice President Walden, of the drone strike which killed 83 children, including Abu Nazir's son, Issa, in a *madrassa* (school). "You realize he's not a good guy," notes Cuesta. "He's not a mustache-twirling bad guy. And the way David played him, you could see he's just a flawed human."

Those flaws also include cheating on his wife—with Carrie. "I remember telling Claire, 'He strikes me as the kind of guy that would tell his wife he's having an affair,'" Harewood recalls. "Carrie must have freaked out and run away, just as Estes told his wife he was in love and had met the girl of his dreams. He put all his eggs in one basket, and that basket was Carrie. That really hurt him, and is one of the reasons he closes Carrie down so much. He's not prepared to let

that girl in." Apparently those feelings never left completely. "He also sees her attraction to Brody, her fascination with him. And he's incredibly jealous."

Estes, along with nearly 300 others, is killed in the massive explosion at the memorial service at the CIA for Walden—an event that was as much a surprise to Harewood as it was for the audience. He began getting a sense something was amiss during the weekend before the 2012 Emmys, during a break in production of "Two Hats."

"We were all in L.A., and I remember feeling something wasn't quite right. Nobody would look me in the eye." A few days later, the actor received a call from Alex Gansa's assistant, explaining that the producer wanted to talk to him about "script developments." "I just knew. And it was very disappointing."

The disappointment didn't stop with the cast. "Usually, when a character gets written off a show," Johannessen explains, "you get a polite response and then, the next day, a seven-page email describing why they should get a much bigger part. David didn't do that—but everybody else did, on his behalf."

The crew members—particularly the female ones—were so upset about losing Harewood that they quickly began a "SAVE NO. 5" campaign (based on Harewood's cast ID number on daily call sheets).

	CAST	CHARACTER
1	CLAIRE DANES	CARRIE MATHISON
3	MORENA BACCARIN	JESSICA BRODY
4	MANDY PATINKIN	SAUL BERENSON
5	DAVID HAREWOOD	DAVID ESTES
6k	MORGAN SAYLOR (k)	DANA BRODY
7k	JACKSON PACE (k)	CHRIS BRODY
8	DEIGO KLATTENHOFF	MAJ. MIKE FABER
11	RUPERT FRIEND	PETER QUINN
16	MAURY STERLING	MAX
16	JAMES URBANIAK	LARRY THE POLYGRAPHER
17	TBD	INTERROGATOR
21	F. MURRAY ABRAHAM	DAR ADAL
23	VALERIE CRUZ	MAJ. JOY MENDEZ

VICE PRESIDENT
WILLIAM WALDEN

SOMETIMES POLITICIANS ARE DRIVEN to do the wrong things for the right reasons. Others are just plain driven and simply do the wrong things.

Actor Jamey Sheridan, who plays Vice President William Walden, sees the Veep, who is the former head of the CIA, this way: "He was a young CIA field agent, who, as the years went by, became more and more jaded." While serving in Afghanistan, Walden had seen a Robin Hood–type revolutionary, Ahmad Shah Massoud, slaughtered, and this put a permanent kink in his moral sense. "That assassination turned him into someone who's willing to murder 83 children to get to the bad guys," says Sheridan, referring to Walden's drone strike, which killed Nazir's son, Issa.

"The way Walden sees it," the actor notes, quoting his character, "'those sons of bitches are hiding behind those kids. If you're hiding behind mama's skirt, and you're killing men, women, and children in my country, I'm going to kill your mama, and then I'm going to kill you.' He has no hesitation about it at all. And he's 100 percent committed."

Walden absolutely believes in what he's doing, says writer Alex Cary. "This is his purpose in life, to keep America safe, and he feels entitled in that. He doesn't understand why anybody thinks that what he does is not correct," including keeping such actions a secret.

Sheridan was originally brought in on recommendation from director Michael Cuesta, to appear in the pilot episode, where his role was simply to greet the returning Brody at Andrews Air Force Base. "Then they told me he'd be recurring," the actor recalls. "It wasn't until the second half of the first season that I really got to begin evolving him," bringing a combination of weakness of character and vicious arrogance to the politician. "That's a messy mix," he laughs.

"Jamey brought a ruthlessness and arrogance to the man, which we hadn't even personalized too much in the scripts," Cary notes. "He nuanced him with those qualities. But Walden's behavior is not evil, because it is rooted in belief. He's not so different from Nazir—they're both fanatics on either side of the same fence."

VIRGIL AND MAX

IF THERE IS ONE SET OF CHARACTERS that make audiences smile on *Homeland*, it's surveillance experts Virgil and his brother, Max. By the way, Virgil *what*? "Nobody knows his last name," remarks actor David Marciano, who plays the techie. "It's top secret."

According to Marciano (per a backstory created by Marciano, Alex Gansa, Michael Cuesta, and Claire Danes, during rehearsals), Virgil graduated with an engineering degree from New Jersey Institute of Technology. "He applied for a job with the CIA and got turned down—by Saul," the actor notes. Virgil is not a subversive of any sort. "He's really just out to make a living. Carrie uses Virgil and Max because they're good and they're cheap." Notes Cuesta, "Virgil has principles, he won't do just anything. And he wants to get paid."

Virgil is considered to be somewhat on the fringes of the CIA, writer Alex Cary says. "It's not entirely clear if he's a CIA operative, a free-lancer, or if he's just dedicated to Carrie and her operations." He's somebody whom Carrie asks to break the law whenever she sees fit. "He's this slightly dodgy character, but he has an extreme affection and loyalty to Carrie, which sort of overrides everything else," says Cary.

He's essentially a big brother to her, says writer Chip Johannessen. "Carrie is so isolated at the CIA. So we wanted to give her some people to have relationships with outside the agency, people who cared about her."

Alongside Virgil is his quirky brother, Max, played by Maury Sterling. "Max is considered to be on the autism spectrum, kind of a savant," Marciano explains. "I bring him along because he sees things that I can't. He has a perceptiveness that goes beyond ordinary human capacity. Max can hear the sirens before they're close enough for me to hear them."

The two offer the show a bit of comic relief in their odd brotherly banter. "Their communication is not entirely functional, which is funny, given they deal with communication," says Cary. "It's this bizarre, close yet distant relationship between two oddball characters who don't quite fit in the same room—let alone in a small van."

FILMING HOMELAND

FILMING IN CHARLOTTE

UNLESS YOU'RE FROM THE Washington, D.C., area, it's hard to imagine that *Homeland* isn't filmed there. But, with only a few exceptions, the series is actually filmed in Charlotte, North Carolina.

North Carolina was chosen because it offers two modest production hubs, the biggest being the seaside town of Wilmington. "Whereas Wilmington has the infrastructure for long-form projects, with studios, facilities, and a crew base," says producer Michael Klick, "Prior to our arrival Charlotte was really set up only for work of a commercial nature." But the smaller city was chosen as the better location for the show because of its environment and its architecture.

"Wilmington is a coastal river community," Klick adds. "It sits on a coastal plain with tall, long-needle pines and sandy soil. Whereas, Charlotte has an urban core, and flora and fauna much like what you would see in Virginia, Maryland, and Washington, with all hardwood and deciduous trees. And it's got beautiful neighborhoods that are very similar to Washington's suburbs inside the Beltway." Charlotte has many beautiful homes to make use of as locations, for places such as the Brodys', Saul's, Maggie's, and Estes's houses, among others, many of them close to each other in the southeastern part of town. Places such as the historic Duke Mansion have been used a number of times. The Duke Mansion became the Vice President's residence in the first two seasons.

Federal architecture, though, is fairly rare in Charlotte. "That's one of our biggest challenges," says production designer John Kretschmer, himself a native of the region. "Charlotte has very little to offer in terms of Washington's scale or structure." One building used often for its federal appeal is the Mecklenburg County Courthouse in downtown Charlotte, which served as the exterior for the State Department, where Elizabeth Gaines is killed in Season 1's "Marine One." The old U.S. District Court, ten blocks to the west, has appeared as the Pentagon interior and a judge's chambers.

The town of Mooresville, to the north of Charlotte, has been used for countless locations in *Homeland*, from Gettysburg ("The Vest") to a mountain-cabin getaway ("The Weekend"), even subbing in for Texas, Mexico, and rural Indiana, all during Saul's trip with Aileen Morgan in "The Weekend." "We shoot in Mooresville quite often," says Kretschmer. "There are plenty of times you'll hear us start out the day in the scouting van, going, 'Ugh, we're going back to Mooresville, huh?'" he laughs.

With an absence of true soundstages for interior sets, the *Homeland* crew decided to build their own. About 100,000 square feet were required. Klick and his team located a 94,000-square-foot warehouse a few miles north of downtown Charlotte and converted it into a complete production facility. "We looked at probably a dozen places and narrowed it down to three or four," he recalls. "The warehouse we chose had been subdivided and rented to different tenants but was empty."

Kretschmer and construction coordinator Roger Scruggs did as they had done previously on shows such as *Army Wives*, converting the building into a combination of offices and soundstages, building in the infrastructure of a full-fledged film production studio. Notes Klick, "There are offices for the directors, locations, assistant directors, and wardrobe at one end of the building. And at the other is the art department, set dressing, graphics, computers, and props," with two soundstages in the center.

Crews worked round the clock to complete the renovation. They not only converted the structure, installed air conditioning, cabling, and electrical systems, but also constructed key sets. "Five weeks after they put the keys in my hand," says Klick, "we were shooting in the Brody house."

The stages house both one-off sets, used in single episodes, and standing sets, such as those for the complete Brody-home interior, Carrie's apartment interior (both upstairs and downstairs), and the CIA interiors, including Saul's and Estes's offices and the Operations Room. Residence interiors other than those just mentioned are filmed at residential locations. Unbeknownst to most viewers, Saul's house was actually filmed at three different locations over the years, due to changes in availability. "If the story's good, and ours are always engaging, you never need to explain a discrepancy," says Kretschmer. "The audience will forgive you."

Camera operator Bob Newcomb and stunt coordinator Cal Johnson prepare to capture the action as Damian Lewis punches a reporter (Dan Mengini) in the backyard of the Brody house location in Season 1's "Grace."

THE BRODY HOUSE

MUCH OF THE DRAMA OF *HOMELAND* takes place at the Brodys' fictional home at 3319 W. Chapman Street in Alexandria, Virginia. The real house, though, like every other location on *Homeland*, is actually 300 miles to the south, in this case in the suburban neighborhood of SouthPark, six miles south of downtown Charlotte.

While the pilot script originally called for the Brody house to be a classic colonial, director Michael Cuesta saw a ranch house as a much better fit. "I really wanted a ranch, because it's more like a labyrinth, with all those hallways," allowing for continuous shots as scenes progress. Hallways are a good thing for a family drama, agrees production designer John Kretschmer, who grew up in such a house not far from the *Homeland* stages. "Those hallways provide for a lot of close interactions and good dramatic tension. If you're mad at your parents, you can storm off down the hall to your room."

After a lengthy scout, Cuesta and Pilot production designer Patti Podesta found their venue in a home designed by architect John A. MacCartney, built in 1930. For the pilot shoot, the house was given a tune-up—complete with new cabinets, countertops, and appliances for the kitchen, and new paint and carpeting. "We tried to keep it a 1980s feeling," Podesta explains. "One of the ideas was that this had been Brody's mom's house, and they had moved into it, and then she died while he was away."

Once the show was picked up, the house's interior was reconstructed, with some modifications, on the stage facility. The set omits the wall between the kitchen and the family room, which opens up the space. "It really allows for more dramatic sightlines, a more cinematic look," Kretschmer notes.

The set retains the original eight-foot-high ceilings of the real house, something that was important to Cuesta. "I wanted those low ceilings. I wanted it to feel slightly claustrophobic for Brody, almost like the house is a prison to him." A set so designed, without the ability to light from above with stage lighting, required cinematographers Nelson Cragg and David Klein to light it with "practical" lighting—such as real lamps and other fixtures—adding yet more realism. Adds Kretschmer, "The low ceilings sell it as a real house. And that's a quality of all of our *Homeland* sets—our sets look real."

The ceilings aren't too real though. "Ours actually lift up when we're not using them, something the fire department required, so that the sprinklers can protect the sets," Kretschmer explains.

The original house has a carport behind the house, accessible from the kitchen, but no garage. The garage in which Brody secretly prays as a Muslim was designed and built onstage.

The production continues to use the Brody House location for any exteriors required (both front and back yards). It also continues to shoot in its front foyer, though for any interiors beyond that it makes use of the standing stage set. "Our set is a close enough match that when we go to the location, we can bring someone in the front door and then turn around and continue the shot on our set," the designer says.

Once the set was completed, and filming was due to begin the following morning, set dresser Summer Eubanks informed Kretschmer that the kitchen needed one final touch—a butcher block kitchen island. Eubanks was in luck. Kretschmer was sitting outside his 1972 Airstream trailer, looking at the perfect candidate. "I have one outside my Airstream, which I use as an outdoor table. I loaded it up in the car the next morning, and it landed on set at 5:30 A.M., and it's been the centerpiece of that kitchen on the series since."

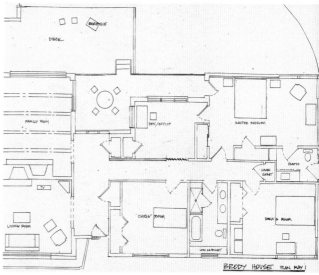

TOP: The original kitchen inside the Brody house location.

MIDDLE: Pilot production designer Patti Podesta's original layout for the Brody home set, based on the location house. A garage was added, not featured in the real house.

BOTTOM: The final set, as built on set at the *Homeland* stages.

CARRIE'S APARTMENT

CARRIE LIVES IN A SIMPLE TOWNHOUSE apartment in the Adams Morgan section of Washington. "It's fairly sparse," pilot production designer Patti Podesta says of Carrie's abode. "She had been demoted about a year earlier and had come back from the Middle East. There's still stuff in boxes. Carrie's not the kind of person who necessarily puts everything away." Notes director and executive producer Michael Cuesta, "She doesn't know how to be home. Every time she's home, you get the sense she'd much rather be out in the field."

The original location used was actually two locations—one for the exterior and another for the interior. The exterior is a townhouse in downtown Charlotte, still used by the production for shots of Carrie entering and leaving her home.

The interior was originally a separate location in SouthPark, six miles to the south (just half a mile from the Brody house location).

Production designer John Kretschmer later rebuilt it on the *Homeland* stage facility. The set retained a small patio off the living room. "We redesigned it to reconcile the two different types of architecture—colonial for the front and modern for the interior," he explains.

The sunken living room/dining room is clearly not set up for chilling on a Sunday watching football with friends. The dining room, in fact, functions as Carrie's home office, something that, as a CIA agent, she's not supposed to have. Her dining room table is her desk, and she has a corkboard containing CIA documents, where she tracks her subjects—mostly Abu Nazir.

The images on the corkboard seen in the pilot were assembled by Podesta, culled from stock photos and other materials. "I went through and made little backstories about the people you're looking at," she explains. "Some of it's surveillance pictures, with different

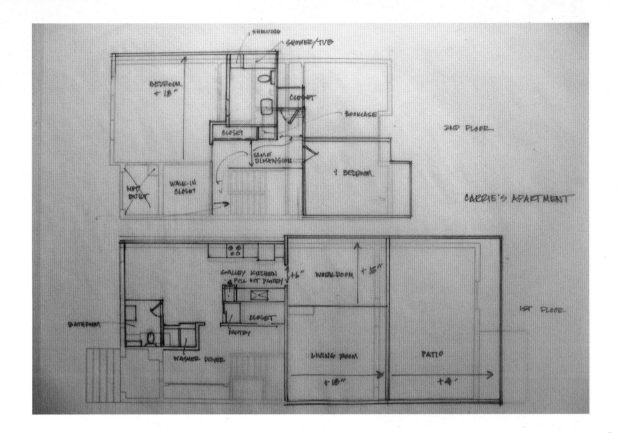

sightings—Baghdad on one side, Afghanistan on the other," complete with dates with which Carrie tracks their movements.

The apartment's furnishings represent a quick dash to Ikea. A quick dash is all the time Carrie would devote to an "I'll take that, that, and that" shopping trip. As for decoration, there isn't much. "She doesn't *live* there," Kretschmer says. "There's very little personal effects. As part of her spy craft, she keeps her home generic enough so that it can't be compromised if someone broke in. With the exception of that corkboard."

There is artwork that's meaningful to her, reflecting her interest in jazz, as well as her travels as a CIA agent." Photos on the walls of jazz artists, like John Coltrane, and of the Middle East, were gathered and placed by set decorator Summer Eubanks, after consulting with Claire Danes, executive producers Alex Gansa, and Cuesta.

For Carrie, it's not a home; it's just a place to go back to—either to leave, to chase after Brody, or to recover from having done so.

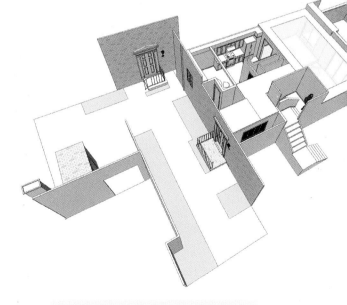

TOP: Pilot production designer Patti Podesta's original sketch showing layout of Carrie's apartment set, overlaid over the original location's design.

BOTTOM: 3-D illustration of Carrie's apartment set by Patti Podesta and art director Christopher Tandon.

THE CIA

FINDING A HOME IN NORTH CAROLINA to represent the Central Intelligence Agency—the nerve center for keeping track of Nicholas Brody and Abu Nazir—wasn't easy. "I had seen some of the location-scouting pictures, and there was nothing," recalls production designer Patti Podesta. "But then our location manager Karl Golden came in and said, 'I think I might have found something.'"

Philip Morris had closed its giant Cabarrus manufacturing facility in Concord, North Carolina, just the year before. Opened in 1982, the 3.6-million-square-foot plant, featuring six enormous manufacturing rooms and countless offices, was the largest cigarette manufacturing plant in the world, at its peak churning out 155 billion cigarettes a year. "It was surrounded by trees and parkland, exactly the way Langley is," Podesta notes. Even the front gate resembled the CIA's.

The production was able to use the facility to stand in for the CIA during filming of the pilot,

but by the time series production began in June, the building had been taken over by a *Hunger Games* shoot, forcing series production designer John Kretschmer to look elsewhere. (*Homeland* would occasionally return to Philip Morris for filming, most notably for the post-blast CIA "morgue" scenes in the Season 2 finale, which were shot in one of the former manufacturing rooms.)

Bringing his daughter, Olivia, in to research the CIA's architecture, Kretschmer and director Michael Cuesta decided to focus not on the CIA's Original Headquarters Building (seen in aerial establishing shots in *Homeland*), but on the more recently built George Bush Center for Intelligence. "It's glass and steel and a little bit more modern and lighter than the brutalist style of the older building," the designer explains. "We thought it might have more legs for the series."

A suitable-looking building was found just eight miles from the Philip Morris facility at the Cambridge Corporate Center in University Research Park. "It has the same glass and steel style of architecture, as well as some other great features," he notes, such as a big, airy atrium, used as the main lobby at the CIA, and wonderful flying walkways, the sites of several key dramatic moments in the series.

In the pilot, David Estes briefs agents about Brody's rescue in a Philip Morris conference room, but after that the key action is set in the Operations Room, the brain center of every tactical operation.

Cuesta wanted the Ops Room to have a subterranean feel. "We wanted to make sure it felt like we were in a basement," Kretschmer explains. "Alex Gansa's term was 'from the ashes,' as if these rooms had been used again and again over the years."

Built as a standing set at the *Homeland* stages, the Ops Room was given a low ceiling, no windows, a raised computer floor, and concrete support columns. "You know you're in a part of the building that's been there awhile."

In terms of equipment, Kretschmer took advantage of research he had done on a visit to a similar "war room" at Fort Bragg, while prepping for his design for *Army Wives*. "There's live video and various communications and electronic services that allow these guys to wage war around the world," he notes.

Interestingly, the main media screens have a classic look, as opposed to something more modern. "We decided to just go with big-screen TVs. While I wanted to make sure we feel like we're seeing a capable spy agency, I also wanted to make sure that we felt the bureaucracy and the lack of funding in some aspects." Kretschmer, in fact, was insistent that the graphics themselves revealed an older Windows XP technology. "I don't want distracting video animation moving at high speed. It feels like yesterday's computers, not tomorrow's computers."

In Season 3, a new location is introduced. The Decommissioned Operations Room allows now-non-agent Carrie to attend the proceedings. "It's in the lower-level basement, in an area that Saul has taken over," Kretschmer says. The room is filled with old equipment, with previous-generation CRT TVs on the wall—that no longer work—and gaps where others have been taken away. "Guys bring in their laptops to run the drone operations. It's one of those rooms where you can still smell the cigarette smoke," Kretchmer notes.

One thing remains clear. "It's not the bugs, electronics, and spyware that make an operation successful. It's the people manning them, as well as the people interpreting the information that comes in. They're the real heroes."

BELOW: Concept drawing by production designer John Kretschmer, showing use of the existing Cambridge Corporate Center lobby as the lobby for the CIA Headquarters building.

THE WRITERS

BEHIND EVERY EPISODE OF *HOMELAND* is a team of some of the best writing talent in television. "They're all really experienced, really balanced and grown up, but also creatively ambitious," says actor Claire Danes.

The writers work together as a supportive team, most often found breaking stories for the show in their Writers' Room in *Homeland*'s offices on the Fox lot. For the first two seasons, that team consisted of six people: Alex Gansa, Howard Gordon, Chip Johannessen, Alex Cary, Henry Bromell, and Meredith Stiehm (Gordon mainly contributed story direction in the beginning of the series, with Gansa continuing as the series "showrunner," continually supervising writing and production and post).

Stiehm moved on after Season 2 to create FX's *The Bridge*, as she had *Cold Case*. Bromell sadly passed away from a sudden heart attack in March 2013, just prior to the beginning of Season 3 (see "A Loss in the Family," page 128). Several additions were made to the team that season, including Barbara Hall, James Yoshimura, Patrick Harbinson, and Charlotte Stoudt.

The process of writing a new season of *Homeland* usually begins with a discussion of the season's story arc, often introduced by Gordon and Gansa. "Howard and Alex had ideas they would bring us, and then we would have a conversation about it, with everyone just throwing out ideas and getting each other's take on them," recalls Stiehm, who returned to cowrite the Season 3 finale with Gansa. "The ideas we liked we then elaborated on."

Gansa keeps the process on track and keeps the show on edge. "He'll often ask, 'Is this really exciting enough?'" Johannessen notes. "He has a clear understanding of how jaw-dropping it should be."

The writers typically work together to map out every scene of every episode. Then the specific task of writing the script for each episode is eventually assigned to one writer or another. "We do all the stories together." explains Johannessen. "So in a certain way, once the story's done, any of us could go off and write it."

The *Homeland* writers office on the Fox lot, known as the Old Writers' Building.

Cary agrees. "For the first two seasons, we were like a band, and we all played our own instruments, and somehow they all played off each other. And every now and again, someone would have a great solo."

The choice of writer is sometimes based on a rotation system or else on a specialty that is needed for the focus of the episode. Cary, for instance, has a military background, having served in the British army. "Because he was a soldier," Johannessen notes, "he not only can contribute a natural reality to military things, but he also has strong opinions of how a soldier like Brody would view things."

Johannessen, a veteran of *24* and *Dexter*, among other series, is strong at building stories, Cary says. "He writes very clearly, with a bullshit-free approach to storytelling. He can detect stuff that makes sense or doesn't track."

Until recently, Stiehm was the only female writer on the staff and could often be counted on to give a proper voice to Carrie. "Meredith's contributions were very much Carrie-centric," Johannessen says. "She was interested in what Carrie was thinking about and doing that was more personal. And because Meredith was interested in it, we were interested in it." He adds, "The way she rendered bipolarity was probably the best rendition of the disorder in filmed entertainment."

Notes Cary, "It really helped inform us and give it authority. It was like instant research having her."

The intelligent and thoughtful Bromell,

beloved by all, brought a specific experience important to *Homeland*, having grown up in the Middle East with a father in the CIA. But it was his ability to get to the heart of a story that enchanted his colleagues. "If we got stuck," Johannessen recalls, "he would go, 'Okay, what do we got?' And he would begin by going, 'Once upon a time, there was a girl named Carrie who . . .' Then he would describe what we were talking about in some way that made it interesting. He'd end with, 'You know what? That's a pretty good story.'"

ABOVE, LEFT: Writer Meredith Stiehm reviews a scene from Season 2's "New Car Smell" with Damian Lewis outside Charlotte's Duke Mansion.

ABOVE, RIGHT: Writer Henry Bromell with director Guy Ferland on the set of Season 1's "Representative Brody" explosion sequence.

BELOW: Writer Chip Johannessen takes a break between takes to chat with director Clark Johnson on location in Puerto Rico during Season 3's "Tower of David" shoot.

SEASON ONE

★ FOLLOWING A LEAD IN IRAQ

while tracking Abu Nazir, the world's most notorious terrorist, CIA Agent Carrie Mathison learns from Nazir's top bomb maker that an American soldier has been turned. Months later, Carrie learns that a Marine, Sgt. Nicholas Brody, missing for eight years and presumed dead, has been found and freed. Her gut tells her that Brody is the turned soldier, but she is unable to convince her superior, Deputy Director David Estes, or her mentor, Saul Berenson, to launch an investigation.

Both men know that Carrie is a brilliant but erratic agent. What they don't know is that Carrie suffers from bipolar disorder, for which she secretly receives medication from her physician sister, Maggie, who also cares for their bipolar father, Frank.

Brody returns home to a hero's welcome, greeted by Vice President William Walden, as well as his wife, Jessica, two children, Dana and Chris, and best friend, Capt. Mike Faber. In Brody's absence, Jessica and Mike have built a relationship, but they quietly put it on hold when Brody returns. Reconnecting with his wife is difficult, but Brody successfully develops a bond with his teenage daughter, Dana.

Although Brody has returned safely, he has to deliver sad news to the wife of Tom Walker, his Marine friend. Tom isn't coming back—he died in captivity. What Brody doesn't reveal is his guilty secret that, forced at the hands of their captors, he was the one who beat his friend to death—or so he was led to believe.

More and more certain of her suspicions about Brody, the tenacious Carrie secretly enlists the help of a surveillance expert, Virgil, and his brother, Max, to set up video surveillance on Brody. When Saul finds out about it, he shuts it down, but Carrie attempts to keep tabs on Brody by following him to a veterans support group and beginning a secretive romance with him.

Saul's Indian-born wife, Mira, returns from a visit home with some difficult news—she has tired of life with her unavailable husband and is leaving. Saul attempts to avoid the sorrow of this by immersing himself in work. He has begun tracking an American-born follower of Nazir's, Aileen Morgan, and her professor boyfriend, Faisel. The two flee after setting up a safe house, which Saul discovers was intended as the base for a sniper planning the assassination of a high-level American politician.

The poker-faced Brody, meanwhile, addresses his fellow Marines at a memorial for Tom Walker. At a reception later at his home, one of his comrades, Lauder Wakefield, begins to question what really happened to Walker. But his rant is interrupted as Brody finally confronts Mike about his relationship with Jessica.

A former guard of Brody's is captured by the CIA, and Saul and Carrie ask Brody to assist in his interrogation. But Brody manages to slip the terrorist a razor blade, and he kills himself rather than talk.

Brody is given a lie-detector test, which, to Carrie's surprise, he passes. Their romance has continued, and she takes Brody on a weekend to her family's cabin, where the two bond. But Carrie lets slip that she's been spying on Brody. She accuses him of being a terrorist and begins to interrogate him. Brody furiously answers her questions but is interrupted when Saul calls Carrie to tell her that he's discovered that Tom Walker is alive and that he's the sniper for whom Aileen Morgan was making preparations. So it appears that Walker is the turned soldier, not Brody. Brody tells Carrie off and leaves the cabin. Angry with Nazir for making him believe that he had killed Tom Walker, Brody confronts a Saudi diplomat accomplice of Nazir's. In response, Nazir's men kidnap and drug Brody, and through his flashbacks, we learn how Brody's relationship with Nazir came about, how he turned Muslim, how he developed a bond with Nazir's son, Issa, who Brody was tutoring, and how the death of Issa in a U.S. drone attack initiated Brody's desire to kill the Vice President, who was responsible for the attack.

Meanwhile, unaware of this history, as is everyone else around Brody, Vice President Walden, wishing to take advantage of the Marine's popularity, suggests Brody run for Congress.

Carrie interrogates the Saudi diplomat and forces him to help the CIA learn Walker's plans, but she is injured in a blast Walker sets off to cover his tracks. While Carrie is hospitalized, she is without her bipolar medication, and her illness is finally revealed to Saul. As Carrie recovers, Saul tries to work out the puzzle of what caused Nazir to lay low for that period. Still manic, Carrie tries to enlist Brody's help in determining what happened to Nazir at that time, but Brody calls Estes, and Estes shuts down Carrie's "research."

Brody and family take what appears to be a simple family vacation to historic Gettysburg. But while there, Brody meets with another Nazir accomplice—a bomb maker who fits him with a suicide vest.

The day before Walden's announcement of his support for Brody's Congressional run, an event that is going to be attended by a healthy chunk of government VIPs, Brody records a martyr video explaining what he is about to do. As the event gets under way, Carrie begins to put the pieces together and tries to stop Brody by warning Saul and then Brody's family.

Working in conjunction with his former comrade, Walker triggers a decoy operation by sniping at the VIPs at the event, forcing Brody, Walden, and the rest through the metal detector at the State Department and into an underground bunker, where Brody is about to set off the bomb. After a failed attempt at detonating the device, due to a malfunction, Brody attempts to set it off once again. But just as he is about to push the button, Dana calls him and begs him to come home, and he abandons the plan.

Her suspicions unproven, and tortured by her mental illness, which has now cost her her career, Carrie decides to undergo electroconvulsive therapy—but not before remembering an important clue—Issa!

"THE PILOT"

HOMELAND'S PILOT EPISODE DELIVERED on its promise of emotional tension, characters that were immediately intriguing, and enough twists and turns to keep audiences wondering—as they would for the remainder of the first season.

Like most TV pilots, *Homeland*'s was filmed entirely on location, in Charlotte and in Israel. In addition to the subtle changes often seen between pilots and series (like final set designs), *Homeland* had a few biggies.

The most important change, as described earlier, was in the Brody family matriarch. In the pilot she was played by Laura Fraser. "Laura Fraser was superb," recalls showrunner Alex Gansa. "She was incredibly soulful. Sort of sad in her depiction of the character," quite different from the Jessica Brody we've come to know. "Someone described her as a meadow creature, with tentative, wide eyes. She did a fantastic job."

Filming was due to begin, with Michael Cuesta directing and cinematographer Chris Manley behind the camera, on Monday,

January 10, 2011, at Charlotte's Freedom Park, with Brody's meeting with Helen Walker. But a freak snowstorm all but shut down production, and the crew abandoned the park location for a few shots at the Brody house location instead. "It was only five inches deep," recalls producer Michael Klick, "but the next morning, we realized it wasn't safe for everybody to get around, so we shut down for two days."

Work continued over what was a sixteen-day shoot in Charlotte, including much work at the Brody house location, most of which would end up being reshot when Morena Baccarin joined the series.

After returning home in the morning—from a date the previous night—Carrie quickly changes from her party girl attire to her work clothes, after giving herself a "whore's bath" at the bathroom sink. "That was added in prep," says director Michael Cuesta. "It's something that sets up that side of her right away, that she's a *Looking for Mr. Goodbar* kind of girl."

Upon arriving at the CIA briefing room (filmed in one of Philip Morris's own conference rooms), Carrie, along with the rest of the team, learns of the discovery of Sgt. Nicholas Brody. Previously missing and presumed dead, he is seen being freed by a Delta Force team from a safe house in the Korengal Valley, Afghanistan.

Scenes taking place in that safe house (including flashback scenes of Brody being tortured) were filmed at a closed dye plant along the Catawba River in northwest Charlotte that belonged to the Clariant Corporation. "I had shown our location manager, Karl Golden, the precise kinds of construction that exist in the Middle East," recalls pilot production designer Patti Podesta. "But those kinds of small, crumbling buildings don't really exist in North Carolina." Golden eventually found the Clariant plant, in which Podesta added some interior partitions, to give Brody a small "cell." She also built a small-scale exterior, constructed mostly from foam, in the parking lot, which the Deltas partially blow up fighting their way inside.

"The factory was due to be demolished, so they let us do whatever we needed," Podesta says. The building remained intact, however, and has been used numerous times in other episodes—most notably as one of Carrie's capture locations by Abu Nazir in Season 2.

The pilot originally contained a scene that was later cut, in which Brody was given a physical exam at Ramstein Air Base (also shot at Philip Morris) by an army doctor, played by actor Brian Robinson. The shaven but long-haired Brody explained the sources of various scars. The one in his left shoulder, he said, was from "a screwdriver. Every couple hours, someone would come in and turn it." (This was shown to viewers in an accompanying flashback.) Regarding another, he noted, "That one hurt the most. Skateboard, when I was fourteen."

Both his family and the Vice President, at Andrews Air Force Base, welcome Brody home. The scene was shot at the Carolinas Aviation Museum, on the grounds of Charlotte Douglas International Airport. After a brief acclimation to life at home, Brody is given a debriefing at the CIA. As seen onscreen, Carrie briefly presses him about his knowledge of Abu Nazir. In the original pilot shoot, she pushes him further, until she is Estes finally stops her. Disturbed, she left the room and fetched her MP3 player from her cubicle (yes, at one time Carrie sat in a cubicle) and quieted herself by listening to jazz.

Showrunner Alex Gansa, director Michael Cuesta, and pilot cinematographer Chris Manley watch a take outside the historic prison at Abu Ghosh on February 10, 2011.

The scene was deleted upon a revisit to the pilot, Danes notes. "We made a decision early on that her breakdowns would happen outside the workplace. We needed to maintain her credibility as a professional officer so that we can accept that she has this condition and also is somehow able to do her job."

Still suspicious, Carrie goes behind Saul's back and sets up surveillance equipment with the help of her old friend, Virgil, and his brother, Max, and begins watching Brody at home. "Not only is the audience watching Brody," Alex Gansa explains, "but the audience is watching Carrie watch Brody. And that makes it more compelling. Because if you begin with Carrie watching him for every clue as to whether he's a bad guy or not, that means every scene he's in, regardless of whether Carrie is watching, it makes the audience wonder."

She watches every aspect of his life, including his private time with Jessica. "A very big influence on this show was a movie called *The Lives of Others*," Gansa says. "It's all about East Germany and the whole surveillance culture that once existed there." The film includes a scene where an intelligence officer is listening to lovemaking going on in an apartment. "You

feel his loneliness as he's listening to two people actually connect with each other. And that's something you see in Carrie, as she watches the same thing."

The love scene in question involves Jessica's first attempt at sex with her husband—a scene that played differently in the original shoot and helped prompt the network to later suggest a casting change. In the original version, it was *Brody* who comforted *Jessica*, as she first reacted to seeing the scars from his torture. Brody gently took things slow, checking on her feelings at each step. In the final pilot, after trying to reassure a nervous Brody, Jessica experiences what amounts to a rape by her husband.

Saul eventually catches up with Carrie at her apartment and, seeing the surveillance gear he had forbade her to use, is furious. To Carrie, rules are an impediment and inconsequential. "She's committed to the company and to her calling," Danes explains, "but her condition has placed her on the periphery. She feels she doesn't have to play by other people's rules. She's reverent to the agency structure and knows it as well as anyone but feels she can afford to break the rules whenever she decides it's necessary."

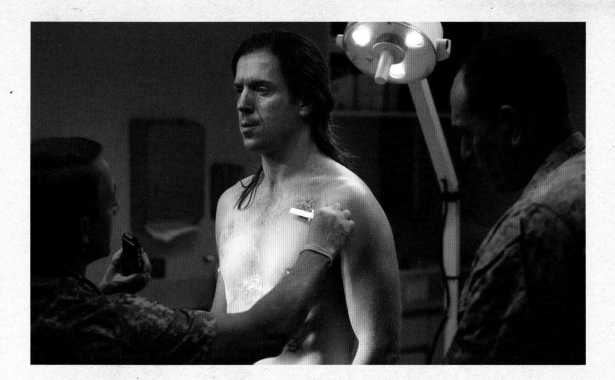

In this case, she pushes it yet further, making a clumsy pass at her mentor, as she would on the outside. "She's played that game in the field so many times, and now all of a sudden, he's a fucking 'asset.' And he's disgusted by it," Cuesta explains. Adds producer Howard Gordon, "He gives her an audience and indulges her cautiously, and she betrays it. And if he feels betrayed by her, we feel betrayed. So by testing the relationship in the pilot, that situated that relationship on such firm ground, in terms of what and who they were to each other."

After wrapping production in Charlotte on January 31, the team spent a day in Washington, filming Lewis on a morning jog around the monuments, eventually stopping before the U.S. Capitol for the iconic ending shot of the pilot. Production then moved to Israel to shoot the opening sequence, in which Carrie gets a tip from Abu Nazir's imprisoned chief bomb maker, Hasan Ibrahim, that a U.S. soldier has been turned. "At first, we were hoping we could find places in Charlotte, or else in L.A.," recalls Podesta. It wasn't until Gideon Raff sent over some images of locations in Israel he had used for *Hatufim* that it was decided to film there.

"We realized we could make a beautiful facsimile of parts of the Middle East here, but nothing could replace the real thing, particularly the people."

Cuesta, Danes, Gordon, Gansa, Klick, and Manley worked for two days, February 9 and 10, in a couple of locations, making use of Raff's *Hatufim* crew. The first day was spent at a historic British prison, a remnant of colonial days and now a museum, in the Arab village of Abu Ghosh, not far from Jerusalem. For those scenes, Podesta had Raff's crew replace the cell/interior doors, to reflect a more recent look, and add appropriate politically inspired graffiti (in Arabic, of course). Several local actors were used, including one, Yousef Sweid, who appears in *Hatufim*, playing the imprisoned Ibrahim.

c Prod.:	Gideon Raff	·	**CREW CALL:**	Weather:	Snow likely, mainly after noon.
d./UPM:	Michael Klick		**7A**	Cloudy with a high near 34 - Chance of precipitation 60%	
ector:	Michael Cuesta		**Shoot Call: 8A**	High: 48	Low: 28

AREST HOSPITAL
olina Medical Center
eville NC 28210

Current Script: YELLOW Rev. 1/5/2011
Current Schedule: GREEN rev. 1/2/1011

Sunrise: 7:32 AM   Sunset: 5:30 PM

SETS ARE CLOSED:
No admittance without prior approval.

All Calls Subject to Change by the UPM or Ads -No Forced Calls without prior Approval of UPM (no exceptions)
NO PERSONAL CAMERAS ALLOWED OR USED ONSET. *ABSOLUTELY NO NON WORKING MINORS ARE ALLOWED ON SET*

SCENES	SETS & DESCRIPTIONS	CAST	D/N	PAGES	LOCATIONS / NOTES
	SAFETY MEETING @ SHOOTING CALL				
0), 62, 64 A66	**EXT BLUEMONT PARK** *Brody waits for Helen, She asks what happened. He says Jessup loved her.*	2, 11, atm	D5	1 4/8	*FREEDOM PARK*
	** ROLL TO VAN**				*CREW PARKING* FREEDOM PARK Park as Directed
60,(62)	**EXT INT. SURVEILLANCE VAN - BLUEMONT PARK** *Virgil & Max work on sound. Carrie watches as Brody meets a woman.*	1,2,9,10,11 atm	D4	1 2/8	
63, (64)	**EXT INT. SURVEILLANCE VAN - BLUEMONT PARK** *Carries sags as she realizes it is Helen Jessup.*	1,2,9,10,11 atm	D4	3/8	
66	**EXT INT. SURVEILLANCE VAN - BLUEMONT PARK** *Virgil confronts Carrie about the mint green pill. (Clozapine)*	1,2,9,10,11 atm	D4	1 6/8	
	COMPANY MOVE TO BRODY HOUSE				
24), 25	**INT BRODY HOUSE - FAMILY ROOM** *Chris & Dana watch the news in their Sunday clothes.*	5, 6	Morn 3	4/8	
rveillance	**INT BRODY HOUSE - FAMILY ROOM** *See surveillance memo for list of the days intended shots and cast needed.*	2,3,5,6			
	** STILL PHOTO SPLINTER UNIT				
1,25,29 photos	**INT PHOTO BACKDROP (Photo Unit)** PHOTOS - 2 Looks - Bootcamp photo, Sgt. Photo PHOTO - Shot of Brody's face to photo shop PHOTOS - Brody w/ 5 year old Dana & baby Chris	2 2 2, atm			
		Total Script Pages =		3 7/8	

CAST	CHARACTER	STATUS	LEAVE	MU	REH	RDY	REMARKS
Claire Danes	Carrie	W	7:45A	8A	9:30A	10A	PU Marriott (fit @loc after shoot)
Damian Lewis	Brody	W	6A	6:15A	7A	8A	PU Marriott
Laura Fraseer	Jessica	W	12N	3P	4P	6P	PU Marriott (fit before MU)
Jackson Pace	Chris (k)	W	3:30P	3P	4P	6P	PU Double Tree (School @ hote 11A
Morgan Saylor	Dana (k)	W	3:30P	4P	4P	6P	PU Double Tree (School @ hotel 11A
Mandy Patinkin	Saul	STR					i
David Marciano	Virgil	SW	8:10A	8A	9:30A	10A	PU Double Tree
Maury Sterling	Max	SW	8:10A	8A	9:30A	10A	PU Double Tree
Afton Williamson	Helen Jessup	SWF	5:45A	6A	7A	8A	PU Double Tree

ATMOSPHERE & STANDINS				SPECIAL INSTRUCTIONS
DESCRIPTION	Report	Set Call	Scenes	
Mother (30s)	6:30A	7:30A	all park scs	**PROPS:** Scs. 60, 62, 63, 64, 66, A66 blankets for lawn(weather permitting), strollers,loaves of bread to feed birds, boom box, Sc 60, 63,66 Carrie's Fieldscope, Surveillance van work table (coordinate w/art dept) Sc 66 Clozapine
Father (30s)	6:30A	7:30A	all park scs	
Female Teens (Urban)	6:30A	7:30A	all park scs	
Joggers	6:30A	7:30A	all park scs	**SET DRESSING:** Sc (24) 25 Family room television, Sc 60, 63, 66 Virgil's Surveillance Van set up, Scs 11, 25, 29 Photo shoot - Marine Flag, U.S. Flag, still backing
Male Teens (Urban)	6:30A	7:30A	all park scs	
Women w/ bike (20 to 40)	6:30A	7:30A	all park scs	
Male w/ bike (20 to 40)	6:30A	7:30A	all park scs	**GREENS:** all park scenes :branches, wild bushes, small trees
Women (20 to 50)	6:30A	7:30A	all park scs	
Men (20 to 50)	6:30A	7:30A	all park scs	**WARDROBE:** Scs 11,25, 29 Photo UnitBrody's Bootcamp Uniform, Brody's Sgt. Uniform, Family photos with small children,
Woman (60s)	6:30A	7:30A	all park scs	
Man (60s)	6:30A	7:30A	all park scs	Scs 24,25 Chris & Dana in Sunday clothes, Chris figits w/ tie, Sc 24, 25 Chris & Dana in Sunday Chris fidgets with tie
5 year old Dana	4P	4:30P	PHOTO	
Baby Chris	4P	4:30P	PHOTO	**GRIP/ELEC** Scs 24, 25 Shoot Night for Day
				CAMERA: Sc 62, 64,A66 Long lens shot (surveillance)
= Total Extras				**VEHICLES:** Scs 60,63,66 Virgil's surveillance van
BG Cars				**All Park Scs:** Golf carts to shuttle, cast , crew & equipment for all scs at park
Carrie SI (Charcol)	9:15A		1st Loc	**LOCATIONS:** Police traffic control, control parking including drive-ways
Brody/Virgil SI	6:45A		1st Loc	
Jessica SI (Blue,Maroon)	3:30P		1st Loc	**PRODUCTION:** Certified Teacher on set
Helen SI	6:45A		1st Loc	
Max SI	9:15A		1st Loc	**FILM/VIDEO:** Sc 60 Virgil's surveillance van computer, green screen, Sc 25 News report to be added Sc (24), 25 Green Screen

oot Day: 2	*Advance Schedule - Tuesday, January 11, 2011*				LOCATIONS / NOTES
SCENES	SET & DESCRIPTIONS	CAST	D/N	PAGES	
42	**EXT INT. STATION WAGON - DRIVING**	2 3 5 6 27	D3	6/8	

Things went smoothly at the prison, but the following day, the crew had a much more harrowing experience while filming Carrie's dash through a busy Arab market when her car becomes stuck in traffic.

The scene was shot on a dead-end street in a village called Barta'a, which straddles both Israeli and Palestinian territory. A local was dispatched with money to compensate the street vendors for the inconvenience of having a film crew invade their market. At first the filming seemed an enjoyable curiosity to the vendors, but "as the day wore on, the magic wore off, and people were getting understandably upset that we were blocking access," recalls Michael Klick. Says Cuesta, "Our contact had paid only one side of the street, and the other merchants were really pissed off. They actually started fighting among each other, but we were afraid they were going to turn on us, so we got out of there in a big hurry." Danes and her husband, Hugh Dancy, were quickly evacuated, followed by Cuesta and his fifteen-year-old son and the remainder of the crew.

Filming completed, the pilot was edited and finished in March. The show had been picked up by Showtime, but after viewing the pilot, the network began having concerns about Laura Fraser's indelibly sensitive performance as Jessica. "What was interesting is that because she was so singular in the role, and because you cared about her so much," says Gansa, "in a crazy way, she detracted from the connection between Brody and Carrie. You wondered where you wanted to focus your attention: were you really rooting for this marriage to get back together, or were you fascinated by this CIA agent's relationship with this supposed terrorist? So in a way, Laura was so good, so sympathetic, that she acted herself out of a job."

Fraser had her fans, of course. "At first, I fought it," Cuesta remembers. "But I eventually understood. Laura was more fragile. Delicate. Complicated. And what we found that we needed was someone who was not fragile and not delicate." That Jessica came in the form of actor Morena Baccarin, fresh from her leading role in ABC's sci-fi series, *V*. Cuesta says,

OPPOSITE: Call sheet from day 1 of production on the *Homeland* pilot, January 10, 2011.

"Jessica is very much the rock of the show. She is the one who has it together. She's willing to put up with only so much, and that's what Morena brought her."

Production began on the new interior sets at the *Homeland* production facility on June 14. Cuesta and team filmed both reshoots for the pilot (scenes including Jessica, as well as other cast members in the original location kitchen) and scenes for the second episode, "Grace." When the exteriors at the original Brody house and the scene of the Andrews welcome were reshot, they had to match the original footage shot in January with snow on the ground. "We ended up having to put fake snow on the ground," Klick describes. "But it was hot." As in ninety-three degrees hot, with cast members dressed as if it were January. "That was awful," Morgan Saylor recalls. "There were only a few outside scenes, but we are all sweating, sweating, sweating."

One of the first reshoots was the love scene between Jessica and Brody. This time around, Jessica attempts to soothe a disconnected Brody, who turns what should be an act of intimacy into something violent and lonely. The camera catches Baccarin in a reaction that reflects a "This is what I waited eight years for?" sense, Cuesta observes. "She gives him that look at the end of the scene, when he's on top of her, like, 'This is not the man that left. This is a different person.' That was what that whole experience was all about." Unlike Fraser's Jessica, Gansa adds, "She was hurt, but she wasn't broken."

It was a tough scene for any actor to play, particularly for one who had just met her costar a few days before the shoot. "In a sense, that ended up working for us, because we were strangers to each other, and we were trying to create a marriage," Baccarin says. "That was the first real hard lesson she learns when he comes home. Whatever it is that he went through and happened to him, it damaged his soul. And that's the first time she really sees it in play." And that was only the beginning.

TOP: The Brodys enjoy a cool winter's day welcome—in June, courtesy of some fake snow.

BOTTOM: Michael Cuesta blocks a shot as Brody is welcomed home at the Brody house location.

SO WHERE WAS BRODY?

Over the course of three seasons of *Homeland*, viewers have had glimpses of Brody's life in captivity over the eight years he was gone, mostly through flashbacks. But screenwriters like to pin things down in order to create a fixed reality for a character. The *Homeland* writing staff thus created this timeline to make sure his story stayed constant.

Brody Timeline

Early 2003	Early 2003	2003	Early 2004	Mid 2004	10 months prior to Brody's rescue	8 months prior to Brody's rescue	Spring 2011
	10 days after capture	2-3 weeks after capture	1 year after capture				
East Iraq/Syrian Border	*Outside Demascus, Syrian Desert*	*Outside Demascus, Syria*	*Outside Demascus, Syria*	*Outside Demascus Syria*	*Baghdad, Iraq*	*Demascus to Afghanistan*	*Korengal Valley, Afghanistan*
Brody & Walker go missing. Interrogation starts immediately inside the secret military facility *outside Demascus, Syria.*	Ep. 101, Sc. 1: (Brody has killed Walker) Brody Buries Walker	Ep. 101, Sc. A10: INT secret military facility: Brody hears whispering outside the door.	Ep. 101, Sc 32: INT secret military facility: Brody has wild hair, matted beard. He's tortured & muttering to himself (talking to Jessica)	Ep. 101, Sc 103-110: INT secret military facility: Brody's hair and beard are longer. He follows the light and discovers his captors praying. They invite him in.	Pilot Episode: Carrie visits her source in jail. He is executed.	Pilot Episode: Brody is smuggled over land to Afghanistan.	Pilot Episode: Secret Military Facility 11PM: Brody is found alive by US Military

THE LOVE TRIANGLE

NOW, THAT'S GOTTA BE HARD: your husband has been missing for eight years and is presumed dead, you end up falling in love with his best friend, and now guess who shows up?

"Jessica does the right thing when Brody comes home," Morena Baccarin says. "She banishes Mike, in a way. He's still in the kids' lives, but she definitely stops their relationship, even though they were on the road to getting married."

No fun for Mike Faber, our favorite stand-up Marine. "They fell in love, and Mike's been there for the family and for Jessica," says actor Diego Klattenhoff, who plays Mike. "And then Brody comes along and throws a wrench in it. So what do you do? You stand down and try to pick up the pieces." And maybe hope that Brody doesn't notice anything.

But Brody does notice. He notices the effect Mike's presence has had on the family. "Brody's an intelligent and emotional guy," says writer Alex Cary, "and I think, at his core, he understands what has happened. And that's a

confusing place to be. His family is alive and has clearly been cared for, and there's clearly been a role model in their lives, a positive one."

So who is the interloper—Mike or Brody? "While Brody waits to get tapped on the shoulder by Nazir to move, what right does he have to sit there with this family whom he loves?" asks Cary. "He's been blindsided by his reconnection with his family. And that's not something in the whole Abu Nazir indoctrination that he saw coming."

Mike and Jessica clearly are the "better couple," in many ways. "Sure they are," says showrunner Alex Gansa. "It's easier, it's simpler. It's not complicated. And you're watching this train wreck of a marriage happen, knowing that this is where it should have gone all the time." Fans, though, often tell Baccarin they've rooted for Jessica and Brody to be together. "I think you see the remnants of the life that was, and you want to take that back," she notes. "But as long as Brody's in their lives, it's going to be a constant struggle."

CARRIE AND BRODY

FANS MAY THINK OF THE RELATIONSHIP between Carrie and Brody as the centerpiece of Season 1 (along with "Is he or isn't he?" of course). But that relationship wasn't always a given.

Early in the season, through Carrie's surveillance of Brody, the seed is planted for something to happen between the two characters. "We needed Carrie to empathize with Brody, during the drama within the drama of Carrie watching what's going on in Brody's house," writer Alex Cary notes. She sees him undress occasionally, kindling an attraction.

But it is not until the fourth episode, writers Gansa and Gordon's "Semper I," that the real spark occurs. Unable to continue her video surveillance, Carrie follows Brody to a veterans support group held in a church basement. The scene was filmed on a warm summer evening in late July at the Sharon Presbyterian Church, a half mile from the Brody house location. The two connect, most notably in their charged conversation in the rainy parking lot.

Lewis and Danes had only one scene together in the pilot, in which Carrie debriefs

Brody upon his return, and the mood was fairly professional. So the energy between the two actors in the parking lot scene came as a surprise. The morning after that scene was filmed, Gansa recalls, "I walked into my office, and my assistant said, 'Alex, you might want to take a look at those dailies.' I said, 'Why, is there a problem?' And she goes, 'The opposite.' I remember watching these two actors together and realizing, 'Wow—this is the show, right here.' So it became clear that we would try to put them in each other's company as often as possible. There was a long story to tell in this relationship."

The question viewers are left asking themselves is, is Carrie just doing her job, or is she crossing the line? "She's sleeping with the enemy," observes director Michael Cuesta. "It's part of her recklessness. She's an addict. And when you're an addict, you know what you're doing is bad for yourself, but you just keep doing it. And that contradiction is very much the engine of the first season—doing what's right for the wrong reasons, and vice versa."

HOW DOES A POLYGRAPH WORK?

Homeland is all about lies and truths. One of the tools intelligence officers use to tell the difference between the two is the polygraph, or "lie detector." We see this machine used in several episodes. But just how does it work?

Thirty-six-year law enforcement veteran Michael "Eddie" Lane serves as *Homeland*'s polygraph consultant. "It's actually a science," he explains. "The examiner is looking for meaningful behavior: eye movement, the wrong words, and body movements that are wrong." The equipment just helps. "It's a good tool. When used properly, it's 93 percent accurate."

The polygraph machine is actually a system made up of a number of instruments that are attached to the subject. Two plastic "pneumograph" tubes attached to the front of the subject's torso measure the subject's breathing. Several electrodermal activity (EDA) and galvanic skin response (GSR) paddles attached to the subject's fingers measure electronic impulses from the brain and activity of the sweat glands. Another device, attached to the subject's middle finger, measures the pulse and provides information on blood volume. Together these instruments all monitor the levels of stress the subject experiences during questioning.

The examiner begins by asking a series of control questions, such as, "Are you in North Carolina today?" Or "Is your name Saul Berenson?" The control questions are followed by relevant questions, like, "Did you kill Tom Walker?" or "Have you ever been unfaithful to your wife?"

Lane explains, "You measure the reaction to a relevant question against the control question," to detect body measurements that change when relevant questions are asked.

So how does someone like Nicholas Brody beat the polygraph? "They don't," says Lane. "They beat the examiner," using countermeasures. "Brody is most concerned about the questioner finding out that he's a converted Muslim or is connected to terrorists, so questions about his faithfulness to his wife aren't going to produce the result that the examiner expects." Brody is also a Marine, and Marines are trained in countermeasures, in case they're captured. So the examiner must exercise skill. Says Lane, "Everybody wants to confess. You just have to give the right reason to do it."

Polygraph expert Michael "Eddie" Lane sets up Mandy Patinkin for a polygraph scene from Season 1's "The Good Soldier."

A LIVING LIE

THE FALLOUT FROM AFSAL HAMID'S martyr suicide in "Blind Spot" continues in Henry Bromell's "The Good Soldier," the only episode directed by *24* veteran Brad Turner. Carrie, Saul, and Estes get a chewing out from CIA higher-up Chip "Shooter" Haigh (played by actor Sherman Howard) about the suicide, prompting the idea of polygraph tests to find out who slipped Hamid the razor blade.

The writers liked the idea of introducing the polygraph, allowing them to combine true-to-life operational content with a peek into their characters' lives. "It was a bit of an experiment," says writer Chip Johannessen. "In the end, though, we realized their personal lives weren't actually that interesting to us, so we pared it down to keep it more charged."

Conducting the polygraph tests is Larry, a technician apparently all too familiar to the agents, and played by character actor James Urbaniak. "He has kind of a cult following," explains casting director Judy Henderson,

mostly from his portrayal of underground comic artist Robert Crumb in the 2003 movie *American Splendor*. "He has a very dry sense of humor. He'll always do something that's not expected."

The cast members found themselves quite fascinated with the lie detector, a $12,000 Lafayette LX4000 polygraph system that belonged to *Homeland*'s polygraph consultant Michael Lane. "They wanted to know everything about what each component did and how it was set up," Lane says. "Mandy really loved the gear—he wanted to know where everything went and what it did." By Season 3, actor Claire Danes was familiar enough with the gear that when Majid Javadi tests her with one in "Still Positive," she was able to tell the props person attaching the device that he had attached one of the plates in reverse.

Brody, the ultimate liar, has no problem beating the polygraph, skillfully passing the "Have you ever been unfaithful to your wife?"

test, the day after having a drunken romp with Carrie. Saul, though, is not so lucky. "He's a nervous wreck," laughs Johannessen. The writers liked the idea that the moral center of *Homeland* couldn't pass a polygraph test. "We thought it would be funny, the idea that he couldn't pass it, but that his mirror, Brody, could lie his way through anything."

Brody also lies his way through a memorial service, lauding his fallen comrade, Tom Walker, all the while remembering beating him to death. The service was filmed at the lovely Avondale Presbyterian Church—a classic white, steepled church near Freedom Park—on a warm summer day in August. "I loved the simplicity of that building," says production designer John Kretschmer. "It's perfect for a memorial, particularly a military one."

At one point, Brody takes a company "roll call" of fellow Bravo Company members, each of whom stands in response. "That's something that really takes place at military memorials," Johannessen points out. The experience was as moving for those on set as it is for the audience. "I got chills when we shot that scene," recalls actor Marc Menchaca.

Menchaca plays Lauder Wakefield, one of the other "voices of truth" in *Homeland*. Crippled by an improvised exploding device (IED), he has both an alcohol problem and a big mouth. "He doesn't hide anything—he's going to tell the truth, and he wants to hear the truth," Menchaca notes. Adds director Michael Cuesta, "He's the one guy who knows the truth," particularly when questioning Walker's death. "But he's a drunk, and that makes him an unreliable truth-sayer. That was the genius writer Henry Bromell brought to him, making him a broken man."

At a reception back at the Brody home, Wakefield tries to get at the truth behind Walker's death and questions Brody's posterboy appearance. He crassly lets his former buddy know that all the guys imagined screwing his wife in his absence, drawing an immediate punch from Mike. But Brody yanks him off and begins pummeling Mike himself. "When he sees Mike jump up to protect Jessica's honor, that's the clue to him that the affair is absolutely true," Johannessen says. That's not his real motivation, notes Cuesta. "It's a way to diffuse the situation, because Wakefield is getting a little too close to the truth about what went on between Brody and Walker. And he doesn't want that to come out."

"THE WEEKEND"

BESIDES THE SEASON FINALE, THERE is no more pivotal episode in Season 1 than Meredith Stiehm's "The Weekend." "It's the moment Carrie and Brody are truly brought together, as lovers and as soul mates," says director Michael Cuesta. "Once you pass that point, no matter what happens between them, there will always be that connection."

While the agent and her quarry escape together to Carrie's family cabin on a lake, Saul takes a long car ride back from Beaumont, Texas, with Aileen Morgan, whom he's apprehended at a bus station on her way to Mexico. Both story lines feature an unlikely pair spending their time together trying to get to know one another, and not solely for personal reasons. Both are about finding out the truth.

"We knew Saul had to get the truth from Aileen," Stiehm recalls. "When the idea of a road trip came up, everybody's eyes in the Writers' Room just lit up. Road trips are ripe for drama. Good scenes and good secrets come out.

And I knew I could make that match up nicely with the scenes in the cabin—these two isolated twosomes."

As for Brody and Carrie, she notes, "We always knew they would disappear together—we planned that. It was time for a good, long day with them."

That trip begins with the pair drinking and shooting pool at a bar, where Carrie taunts some bikers. "It was Chip Johannessen's brainchild to have Carrie mouth off to these skinhead racists, for them to bond over screwing these guys over," Stiehm notes. The scene was shot at the Fat Parrot in northern Charlotte. "It's a well-known dive," laughs production designer John Kretschmer. "It was a biker bar in its day, of noted ill repute."

Later the same day the couple arrives at Carrie's family cabin. The location used for the shoot, filmed in the last three days of August, was a three-room cabin built in 1965. The structure sits on a finger of land southwest of Mooresville on Lake Norman, which had been created two years before when the Catawba River was dammed. The location, with its woods, lake, and pier, was ripe for drama and romance. (A side trip to Triple Falls in nearby DuPont State Forest, seen in *The Last of the Mohicans*, is mentioned in dialogue but was never filmed due to scheduling difficulties.)

Though Carrie is, of course, "working," the two find themselves building a genuine bond, Stiehm says. "They both have ulterior motives—she wants to get in his head, he wants to find out what this woman's up to. But they find comfort in each other in ways they didn't expect. The feelings sneak up on them as the weekend progresses." Adds Damian Lewis, "You're never quite sure whether two professionals are working each other over, or whether two lovers and intimates are affecting one another."

Unlike Jessica, who is shocked by the sight of Brody's scars, Carrie kisses them while the two are making love. "He's got the physical scars, she's got the psychological scars," Stiehm states. "She doesn't turn away from them, she recognizes them—she's wounded, too." In the warmth of her embrace, Brody stops, telling Carrie, "I just want to live here." Says Stiehm, "He's very raw and bare, and it's kind of extraordinary to be a witness to that."

Meanwhile, Saul and Aileen are on the road. (Mooresville once again subs for the Mexican border and, later, a West Virginia police station). Saul skillfully turns his angry, ice-cold passenger into a relieved informant. He does it in a manner only Saul Berenson can do—by sharing personal details from his own life.

Until the death of her boyfriend, Raqim Faisel, Aileen had seen herself as the consummate soldier. But with his death and her flight, "she's started to unravel and starts making bad decisions, leaving a trail," notes actor Marin

Ireland. "She never thought this would happen to her."

Ireland delivers a perfect performance as the quiet, embittered, captured terrorist, her performance consisting of emotion-filled stares out the car window as Saul picks at her psyche. Says Cuesta, "Marin has an anger about her, able to play 'I have a chip on my shoulder' brilliantly. That's a gift—you don't learn that. I just mounted the camera on the side of the car and watched her." At one point, Patinkin, in an attempt to break the silence, began singing her show tunes.

"It brought up that sensation of sitting in the car with my dad after getting in trouble," Ireland relates. "I didn't have to create it. Saul is so clearly manipulative in everything he's saying—trying to break me—and it just fuels the rage. And in the confines of a car, there's nowhere to go."

The ride was filmed on Highway 3, a country road southeast of Mooresville. Eventually, Saul pulls over and shows Aileen the remains of a makeshift "synagogue" from his childhood, now a run-down shack, and explains to her the sense of isolation he felt as a child, as one of only a handful of Jews in an Indiana farm town. "Visually, it had to be something that hadn't been a synagogue in a very long time," says Kretschmer. "We found it at the end of a road where there was a lovely farmhouse with a shed that was about to fall apart." Set decorator Summer Eubanks placed simple, repurposed furniture, such as hand-hewn benches and a Torah "ark" made from an antique dry sink.

The scene was one of the most difficult for Stiehm to write, she recalls. "I talked to Chip about it, and then Howard put me together with a rabbi." She eventually connected with a family friend of her father's, Dr. Leon Rosenberg, who shared his experience growing up Jewish in fairly un-Jewish Madison, Wisconsin. "He talked about not being able to sing Christmas carols in school, not playing certain games, and just wanting to fit in. And that's essentially Saul's speech."

The effect on Aileen is immense. "It's so unexpected to her that he's sharing this personal

TOP: The view of the beautiful cabin location from Lake Norman.

CENTER: Cinematographer Nelson Cragg (black shirt) and director Michael Cuesta (far right) scout a shot of the cabin from Lake Norman.

BOTTOM: Claire Danes and actress Amy Hargreaves, who plays Carrie's sister, Maggie, relax at the front step of the cabin, in a deleted scene.

Director Michael Cuesta works with Lewis and Danes on a scene in which their characters walk in the woods.

information with her," Ireland explains. "It shows respect for her and puts them on an equal footing. It's so real and private that she knows he's not simply being manipulative. It's so unexpected, that she lets it in."

Saul later gets out of Aileen that Walker is alive, and lets Carrie know that Walker, apparently, is the soldier who was turned, not Brody. Carrie, meanwhile, has had her chance to ask Brody the "tough questions," and he's told both Carrie and the audience the things they've been waiting to hear him say all season: he killed Walker, he is a Muslim, and, yes, he knows Nazir. "It becomes an interrogation, but in a different setting," says Stiehm. She asks him every question the audience has been wondering about." Adds Cuesta, "It's one of the reasons that episode

works so well. We focus on them, they both have their secrets, and the secrets are revealed."

Once Carrie believes—for the moment—that she was wrong about Brody, he gives her a perfectly delivered, "Carrie, fuck you." "At that moment," says Stiehm, "Brody has it together. 'Fuck you, you're a liar.' He also begins to wonder, 'What am I doing?'"

Brody returns home to his sleeping family and begins to cry. Says Cuesta, "He realizes there's so much at stake here. It will kill his family if he goes through with it. Plus, he's falling for Carrie."

The revelation that it was Walker who had been turned, not Brody, was, from the beginning, supposed to have been the end of Season 1's story arc. "The idea was that the audience is sure about Brody, and then we turn it on its head with this revelation about Walker being alive," Stiehm explains. "But we ended up burning through that much earlier in the season. To Alex Gansa's credit, he bravely let us eat up that story early, knowing we would have to start from scratch and come up with more." The blank slate would soon be filled.

ABU NAZIR

EVERY HERO NEEDS A NEMESIS. CARRIE
Mathison's is Abu Nazir. "He's the great white
whale to her Captain Ahab," *Homeland* executive
producer Howard Gordon states. Nazir is the
spearhead of the threat against America, and
Carrie will do anything to stop him.

Actor Navid Negahban bumped into Gordon,
who was doing a public book reading of Iranian
poet Sholeh Wolpe, and, having read the pilot
script, asked Gordon if the character had been
cast. Not long after, Negahban came in to read
for Gordon and Alex Gansa. Gansa asked him
what he thought about Nazir. "I said, 'To be
honest,'" the actor recalls responding, "'he's a
husband, he's a teacher, he might have been a
politician. He's someone who wanted to better
his country, and now he's in a situation that
he has to react to, and is doing what he sees
needs to be done.' I didn't want to brand him
a terrorist. I just wanted to play the man. And
Alex and Howard looked at me and said, 'That's
exactly where we want to go with him.'"

Negahban gave Nazir a spin that other
actors might have missed. "Navid brought a

human being to this," says writer Alex Cary. "He
made the issue of 'What is a terrorist?' more
interesting than just a guy with a bomb and an
evil mind;" something, he notes, that can be a
tricky matter to deal with. "We always want to
be careful not to humanize terrorists, but you
have to get behind character motives, and that's
what Navid did."

While, to the audience, Nazir may appear
merely a master manipulator, particularly with
regard to Brody, Negahban saw him otherwise.
"To me, Abu comes from a place of love," the
actor states. "He has love for his country, love
for his son, love for his beliefs."

"In Brody, he found someone for the first
time who was pure, someone who could be
a messenger." Nazir, Negahban says, is like
a father to Brody. "And there are two sides to a
father, a strict father and a loving father. The
strict father says you have to do your homework,
and if you don't do your homework, you're in
trouble. But at the same time, if he sees that
the son has fallen and scraped his knee, he will
sit down and take care of his knee. Both sides
are there with Abu."

Nazir and Brody truly bonded, he says,
when, during the pilot, Nazir comforts the

> "To me, Abu comes from a place of love . . .
> [Homeland] allows the audience to think for themselves
> about who is a good guy and who is a villain."
> — NAVID NEGAHBAN, Abu Nazir

crying Brody, while forcing him to beat his comrade, Walker. "In that moment, Damian broke down, and I couldn't stop myself and took him in my arms, which was not in the script. That was the birth of the connection between the two men."

While the writers appreciated Negahban's benevolent approach, Gansa notes, "Howard and I would talk to him and say, 'Look, the guy is a terrorist.'" Cary agrees. "Navid's right to look at it from the pure narcissism of a terrorist trying to humanize what he's doing. But we're telling a story about a guy who mind-fucks somebody, and then uses him as a weapon against America."

Nazir, Cary says, created an illusion. "By stripping Brody down to the studs, he was able to create an illusion of this father figure in Brody's mind's eye." Adds director Michael Cuesta, "Brody now has no moral compass. The north pole is now Abu Nazir."

Playing a terrorist has its advantages. "When I'm at the security checkpoint at the airport, they sometimes pull me out of line and put me on through," Negahban laughs. "One of the agents once looked at me and asked 'What do you do for a living?' I said, 'I'm an actor. Lately, I've been playing the most wanted terrorist on TV.' He got a big smile and then turned to his colleague and said, 'Abu Nazir is here!'"

Even more important to the actor, though, is the reaction from those viewers in the Middle East who see that he has tried to portray something more complicated than the caricatured terrorist. "I was sitting in a coffee shop in Israel, and a guy just came up and shook my hand and thanked me," Negahban says. "*Homeland* doesn't give anybody an answer, it raises questions. And it allows the audience to think for themselves about who is a good guy and who is a villain."

"CROSSFIRE"

FLASHBACKS HAVE ALWAYS BEEN PART OF *Homeland*'s visual language, and in "Crossfire," episode 9, writer Alex Cary uses flashback to show the defining incidents that have led Brody to where he is today. The narrative these flashbacks reveal was designed to take the audience deeper into Brody's motivations, beyond the basic question, is he a terrorist or not?

After five years of keeping him in solitary captivity, Abu Nazir brings a bedraggled Brody to his mountain villa to have him serve as teacher to his ten-year-old son, Issa. Why Brody? "Abu sees strength in him," says actor Navid Negahban. "Who better than a strong man, my enemy who became my friend, who was strong enough to challenge me, to teach my son to become a strong man?" The story parallels one found in *Prisoners of War*, in which terrorist Jamal brings Israeli captive Uri out of his cell to teach his son math.

Issa was played not by a ten-year-old, but by six-year-old Rohan Chand. Recalls casting director Judy Henderson, "Rohan was very real. He was very smart, and he liked pretending and was able to follow direction." With his wide eyes and soulful, innocent face, Cary says, "he had an inherent wisdom to him." Adds Henderson, "There are children who are actors, but then there happen to be actors who are children. That's this little boy."

Chand also brought a wonderful Arabic accent, rolling his *r*'s in a charming manner as Brody teaches him "Take Me Out to the Ball Game." "Rohan came up with that. That was one of the things he read at his audition," Henderson states. Like all child actors, Rohan had his father accompany him on set; and their bond didn't go unnoticed. "The two of them had this very close, tender relationship, which both Damian and I watched on set," Cary notes. "It was touching to see, and we kind of stole from it a little bit."

Cary also borrowed from his own life, particularly his relationship with his two sons.

"My eldest son is now eighteen, and I had taught him to play soccer and coached him for years," much the way Brody does with Nazir's son.

Another child character, Ahmed (played by actor Alex Maier), son of the Saudi diplomat to whose house the kidnapped Brody is taken, was filmed with Lewis on the "White Room" set, in the scene where Brody lapses in and out of consciousness before flashing back to Iraq. Meant to trigger his memories of Issa, the scene was later cut.

The scenes at Nazir's mountain villa, which take place over a year's time, were filmed in an abandoned gas station. "We were struggling to find the right kind of architecture in Charlotte," production designer John Kretschmer recalls. "Then a light bulb went off: a gas station would be the exact type of building we needed." With time running out, Kretschmer happened upon just such a structure on Rozzelles Ferry Road in Charlotte with a "for sale" sign out front. "I went back to my office, and by 6 P.M., I had renderings ready. We found it on a Monday, and it was built and ready to shoot the following Monday," complete with a library, a bedroom, a bathroom—and an exterior courtyard, which Kretschmer added.

During one of the two days of filming at the location with Lewis and Chand, a thunderstorm occurred, forcing electrical equipment to be shut down for two hours, for safety reasons. "We lit the scenes with iPhones and cigarette lighters," Cary recalls. "It worked really well."

The drone strike Walden orders on Issa's madrassa (school), killing eighty-three civilians, many of them children, including Issa, was filmed at the site of the abandoned East Coast Bible College. Located off Wilkinson Boulevard, just north of Charlotte Douglas Airport, the building had suffered a large fire in 2004, making it a perfect set for a scene depicting a bomb's aftermath. "It's got rusted, bent girders hanging down, and the roof is missing," says Kretschmer. Adds producer Michael Klick, "We had been scouting it ever since the pilot, trying to find a place to put it to good use." With the addition of smoke, handheld camera, and several amputee extras, a horrific scene results.

Lewis experienced the scene more personally, working with his young costar, the actor notes. "Picking him up out of the rubble, on the day that we shot all of that, was heartbreaking, was very distressing."

Prior to the strike and the loss of Issa, Nazir had never considered the possibility of turning Brody. "If the strike hadn't happened," showrunner Gansa explains, "Brody would have just been a prisoner for the rest of the war. It was the death of Nazir's own son, and Brody's reaction to it, that led Nazir to be opportunistic and use it to guide Brody to do what he does." It is Nazir's words, after the two view Walden's comments blaming Nazir for the pointless deaths, that push Brody over the line. Nazir says, "And they call us terrorists." "That really pissed off the right-wing bloggers, which was actually my intention," recalls Cary. The writer drew on his own military experience dealing with terrorists in Northern Ireland. "It was interesting for me to write that line, because I obviously don't

agree with terrorism, but, in my experience, it helps to understand the human reasons behind what terrorists do."

Brody and Nazir are companions-in-grief over Issa, something that creates a shift in their relationship, although it doesn't necessarily put them on the same side. "Brody's not an idiot. I don't think he ever wanted to be a terrorist," says Cary. "I think all he wants is to be honest to himself, particularly after hearing Walden."

OPPOSITE TOP: Actor Rohan Chand (Issa) poses with his "dad," Navid Negahban (Abu Nazir), on the location of the Nazir mountain villa, September 26, 2011.

OPPOSITE BOTTOM: A scene from "Crossfire" showing the completed set.

ABOVE: Brody absorbs the effects of the drone strike on Issa's madrasa a half mile away, while sitting in the library of the Nazir villa.

AN EXPLOSION IN FARRAGUT SQUARE

IN HENRY BROMELL'S "REPRESENTATIVE Brody," Vice President Walden asks Brody to consider running for Congress, to fill the seat of shamed "sexter" Rep. Dick Johnson (whose scandal was modeled after that of Anthony Weiner). This will help keep Brody's own mission on track, but first he must get his family on board.

Saul and Carrie meanwhile follow up on Mansour Al-Zahrani, the Saudi diplomat to whose house the kidnapped Brody was taken in "Crossfire." Finding plenty of dirty laundry on Al-Zahrani, they lure him to his bank, Carrie interrogates him to force his cooperation.

TV veteran Guy Ferland (*The Walking Dead, The Shield*) directed the episode. Ferland had worked with Bromell before, and was a great fan of the writer. "We would hang out on weekends, have dinners," the director recalls, "and he'd have these moments where he'd suddenly say, 'I was up all night, and I have an idea for that sequence you're shooting Monday.' He was a

great collaborator." Ferland would also direct Bromell's "Broken Hearts" in Season 2 as well as Chip Johannessen's "A Gettysburg Address."

A quality to Bromell's writing, Ferland notes, is the presence of long, key scenes. "His episodes always have long operatic set pieces in them with big emotions and big production value." "Representative Brody" was no exception, featuring two such scenes.

The first, the interrogation of Al-Zahrani, was shot in seven-minute takes between Claire Danes and actor Ramsey Faragallah, who plays the diplomat. "Claire is very comfortable with long scenes, because of her theatrical training," the director states. "And whenever there's an actor, like Ramsey, with a lot of stage experience for Claire to be up against, it's fantastic."

The straight-laced Faragallah's main concerns were in playing a diplomat with gay leanings. "He's very proper," notes casting director Judy Henderson. "When he read the script, he said, 'Oh—my family!'" she laughs.

Ferland explained to Faragallah how the coverage of the compromising shots of Al-Zahrani engaged in unconventional activities (shot at a Charlotte night club called Butter) would be made, and this assured the actor. "He was fine with it," Ferland notes.

One of the actor's most memorable lines, making reference to oral sex ("Yummy, yummy, yummy!"), delivered with perfect sarcastic anger (per direction from Ferland) also inspired some musical play. A crew band, which includes director Michael Cuesta, adopted the phrase as their band name.

Filmed on an empty floor of the then-new NASCAR headquarters building (also home to the Charlotte Regional Film Commission) in downtown Charlotte, the sequence represents an important turn in Carrie's relationship with Saul, whose interrogation techniques she successfully implements with Al-Zahrani. "It's really a teacher and mentor scene," Ferland notes. "It's spy craft that feels truly authentic, wearing someone down without physical force. A real testament to the writing."

The second of Ferland's long scenes in this episode is a complex explosion scene, in which Tom Walker blows up a briefcase bomb in Washington's Farragut Square, filmed at Marshall Park in downtown Charlotte. "The challenge there was to find a location that would allow for sniper surveillance and three points of view," explains production designer John Kretschmer. "Marshall Park worked well for a generic downtown city park." Washingtonians may grumble about its unfederal look, but that style of architecture is difficult to find in Charlotte. "I'll 'take the letter' on that one," he laughs (referring to an industry term for accepting fans' comments).

Ferland carefully orchestrated the sequence, which filmed over two days, on October 3 and 4, to allow it to be filmed essentially in real time. He spent hours rehearsing with all of the cast and extras. "I actually gave Claire a working earwig, so that all the lines that she needed to respond to she could hear in her ear while playing the scene," the director explains. "I could have her walk through the whole sequence;

it was all there for her. All it needed was a great actress in the middle of it, which we had."

Danes even was involved in the physicality of the explosion, performing everything except one shot. "She did everything except the shot of her flying through the air," which was performed by her regular stunt double, Abigail Martin. A total of sixty extras were used, including two "burned civilians" (one of whom was actually the show's primo stunt coordinator, Cal Johnson, who was lit aflame for the scene).

OPPOSITE: Stunt performer Peter King sets *Homeland*'s stunt coordinator, Cal Johnson, aflame for the bomb aftermath sequence.

BELOW: Stunt performer Abigail Martin goes "on the fly" for Claire Danes in the briefcase bomb explosion scene.

A TRIP TO GETTYSBURG

BY THE END OF "THE WEEKEND," AUDI-ences were still wondering "Is he or isn't he?" It had been revealed that Tom Walker was alive and had been turned, and at that point the writers were at the end of their original story plan, as it had been laid out at the beginning of the season. So now what?

At the end of the following episode, "Achilles Heel," Brody's true leanings are revealed, as he confronts Al-Zahrani about Walker. "From the beginning," says writer Chip Johannessen, "it had always been a two-pronged attack we were planning," with Brody and Walker working in conjunction with one another. It was just a question of when to let the audience in on it. "We realized it was not a good idea to leave that to the very end. Because a lot of the fun of the show was going to be knowing what side he was on, the idea of actually living with a terrorist."

The viewers still didn't really know, though, says writer Alex Cary. "That's the whole question of Season 1. A married man might think about sex with another woman, but that doesn't make him an adulterer—the same thing with terrorism. Brody's not a terrorist until he actually does something." In "The Vest," directed by Clark Johnson, Brody takes one more step closer to becoming one.

The writing team had been reading a book called *The Triple Agent: The al-Qaeda Mole Who Infiltrated the CIA* by Joby Warrick, part of which detailed the workings of a suicide vest. "The vest was a very Henry [Bromell] thing," Johannessen notes. "He loved those kinds of details."

Not everyone was enamored of the idea, though, particularly the actor who would wear it. "I was very worried about the vest," says Lewis. "I thought, 'Really? We've taken great care to show that he's a Muslim, but he's not a jihadist.' If he committed a violent act, it would be for more personal reasons." Executive producer Howard Gordon agreed. "The idea of a Marine wearing a vest was disturbing. So it had to be personal," he notes. "If we were going to believe that Brody would go ahead and do this, it can't be for some generic ideological reason." The death of Issa and 83 other children, and its subsequent mishandling, would do. The extreme symbolism of the vest also made a difference. "In the end," says Lewis, "I just couldn't argue with the visual power of a suicide vest."

It then became a matter of how to get it to him. Bromell was a great fan of road trips, so in "The Vest," the Brody family takes a trip to Gettysburg. And, once again, nearby Mooresville was used as the location, in particular its small-town downtown area. "I've been to Gettysburg, and downtown Mooresville looks a lot like it," says Johnson, himself a bit of a Civil War historian.

Brody excuses himself ("I forgot my toothbrush") and finds his way to a tailor shop, where he meets with an older, Middle Eastern tailor, played by Egyptian-born Nasser Faris, who has spent the day building the suicide vest. "It's very hard to cast older Middle Eastern characters, because the pool of actors is so small," says casting director Judy Henderson. "But Nasser

conveyed the tailor's methodical nature, and that he's a frightened man who is perhaps being forced to do this." The tailor also smokes—a lot. "I really wanted him to smoke, and so did the actor," notes Johnson. "He's one of those guys that you see that just smokes and works silently. You get your suit back, and it looks beautiful, but it smells like unfiltered Lucky Strikes." Adds Johannessen, "We actually brought that forward into Season 2, where Dana notices the smell in the car and asks Brody about it."

The tailor's back room was actually a set built down the street, but the storefront used was a haberdashery called John Franklin Ltd. on Mooresville's Main Street, which had been at that location for many years.

The director particularly liked the location because of the railroad tracks that ran past the back of the building, which are shown in the episode. "Train tracks are such a big part of small-town America, often running right down Main Street," he describes. "I wanted Brody to come out and walk by those tracks and go meet his family and say, 'Oh, I had to get a toothbrush.'" At one point, a freight

TOP: Before and after shots, showing the Brodys at the Gettysburg Battlefield. The scene was actually shot on the grounds of the Philip Morris building, but with a little help from Lion VFX, was transformed to appear more like the real site.

MIDDLE: Director Clark Johnson explains a shot to Damian Lewis behind the tailor shop in downtown Mooresville. Note the railroad tracks, a favorite cinematic element of the town for the director.

BOTTOM: Damian Lewis and Morgan Saylor enjoy a light moment between takes in Mooresville. The scene being filmed is that in which Brody stops Dana from getting too curious about the package in the trunk.

train came, but Johnson just missed the shot he wanted, with Brody visible between cars. "I ran down the track and asked the engineer if she could back up and do it again, and she did," and Johnson captured the moment perfectly. Brody and his family visit the battlefield site, and Brody tells them the story of the Civil War's Battle of Gettysburg. This scene was filmed not in Mooresville, but along one of the back driveways at Philip Morris, taking advantage of the large, lush property (augmented by Lion VFX to add several hills critical to the battle). A key part of Brody's account of the battle is his mention of Union officer Joshua Chamberlain, who Brody explains was a former schoolteacher who "was willing to do what was necessary to do what he believed in." Brody is, of course, telling his own story. "That's an example of the subtleties of the writing on this show," Johnson comments, "where they can take something out of history and apply it to their own situation. It's genius."

In this scene, Brody spends time essentially saying good-bye to each of his family members, some of whom are more oblivious than others. After her father asks her to watch after her mom, and after he physically stops her from seeing the package he's hiding, *both* of Dana's eyebrows are raised. "She's not suspicious, she's curious," actor Morgan Saylor notes. "I think she thinks something might be wrong with him, or maybe he's leaving." Lewis's performance in this scene had a strong effect on his young costar. "I read that scene as something small, but Damian grabbed my face, and it felt so intense that tears came to my eyes."

Back in the hotel, Jessica and her husband finally truly make love, something which Johnson says is likely partially uncomfortable for Brody. "He knows the horrible thing he's hiding, and he has to make her feel that nothing's untoward," the director says. "But I'm sure he still wanted that intimacy, to share that moment with his wife." It's a happy moment for Jessica. "She thinks things are starting to look up, like the marriage is finally on track," says Morena Baccarin. "And it's heartbreaking, because of what's about to unfold."

BUILDING A BETTER SUICIDE VEST

If a Marine was going to wear a suicide vest on *Homeland*, property master Gillian Albinski wanted to make sure it would look and act like the real thing.

In collaboration with production designer John Kretschmer and costume designer Katina Le Kerr, she began crafting designs in early October. "I was researching it online," Albinski recalls, "and I came across a BBC video that talked about building suicide vests. We all looked at it, and said, 'Yeah, that's the one.'"

Albinski also consulted with Jim Windle, a former Marine and a twenty-three-year veteran of the Charlotte-Mecklenburg Police Department, the sergeant in charge of the agency's bomb squad with expertise in terrorist devices. "Gillian had done a lot of research and had a rudimentary design, and I walked her through how an explosive chain works," Windle says.

The vest made by Brody's "tailor" is a design typical of the Middle Eastern jihadist. Projectiles, such as ball bearings or hex nuts, are glued in place on a piece of fabric and allowed to dry overnight. A layer of explosive is then placed on top, over which loops of detonating cord (a high explosive in rope form) are laid, which sets off the main explosive, much the way kindling is used to ignite logs in a fireplace. A second piece of fabric is stitched to the first so that it envelops the device and creates a panel that will be worn on the front of the body. A small blasting cap is added and connected to a battery via wires. The cap ignites the detonating cord when the wearer throws a small switch.

An identical second panel is to be worn on the back of the body. In both panels, the projectile sides face outward so that the explosion forces the projectiles outward into the crowd of targets.

"The Vest" writer Chip Johannessen originally wanted children's jacks to be used as the projectile, because they would create an interesting visual pattern, but colleague Alex Cary quickly shot down the idea. "I was vehemently against that," says Cary. "I felt it made Brody very, very vicious," and bent more on terrorism than personal revenge. Showrunner Alex Gansa eventually ruled in favor of ball bearings. Confesses Johannessen, "I was moping for a few days."

Ball bearings had two additional advantages: they helped make the prop vest slim enough for Lewis to convincingly wear underneath his uniform, and, as Albinski notes, "They're actually more deadly.

Each one becomes its own little bullet." The tailor who makes the vest is shown pouring ball bearings in place, but they were left out of the costume vest because they would have made it too heavy to wear on set.

Though Albinski's research suggested that a military plastic explosive known as C-4 might be used in the vest, Windle says that is not common. "It's actually too powerful for that use. The idea is not to vaporize the body. They just want to get enough explosive to throw the projectile through their own clothing and into the population." Middle Eastern terrorists, he notes, are partial to homemade explosives, such as very sensitive crystalline TATP (used by shoe bomber Richard Reid), laid in place in a grid of packets, or Russian Semtex, a plastic explosive cousin to C-4, which can be rolled out like cookie dough and placed in a layer.

It's important to the story in episode "Marine One" that the vest fails when Brody initially throws the switch. "That's actually very common," Windle states. "Jihadists typically use scrap wire, so different lengths are twisted together and covered with tape." In the story, Brody has been jostled roughly enough when forced into the building after Walker's sniping that one such connection has come apart, forcing him to make an emergency repair in the bathroom of the bunker. He accidentally pierces his finger with the end of a wire while twisting, a detail improvised by Lewis. "That just added one more layer of credibility."

So how good was the final prop? "Jim Windle looked at it and said, 'If I walked in the room and saw that, I would back out of the room and call the bomb squad,'" Albinski says proudly. It was perhaps a little too real for the crew, particularly the day Brody first tries on the vest at the tailor's. "It was actually very stressful, it permeated everything. It's the first time we realize that Brody has truly been turned."

TOP LEFT: Damian Lewis tries on the suicide vest for the first time at the *Homeland* stages.

TOP RIGHT: Don't blow it: Damian Lewis poses wearing the vest with prop master Gillian Albinski on Season 1's final day of filming, November 9, 2011.

RIGHT: The prop team's workbench, crafting three suicide vests for Damian Lewis to "repair" over multiple takes in "Marine One."

THE RAINBOW WALL

IN "THE VEST," AFTER THE EXPLOSION in Farragut Square, Saul finds Carrie in the hospital and, for the first time, learns of her bipolar condition firsthand. Without the medication she was taking in secret, Carrie is unable to control the symptoms of her illness. While trying to explain to Saul her belief about Brody, Carrie demands a colored pen. And it can't be just any colored pen—she insists on green.

That portion of the episode, as well as the later scene in Carrie's apartment, were written by Meredith Stiehm, whose experience with her own sister's disease (see "The Writers," pages 38–39) helped her create a realistic picture. "People that are manic often think they see signs or symbols, and they often have grandiose thoughts about the meaning of things that to you or me seem mundane," she explains. "When Saul visits her at the hospital, she's so sure that she knows something."

By the end of the episode, Saul is beginning to agree that that is indeed the case. Carrie has assembled a mass of papers, each color-coded with different highlighter colors, to represent different eras of activity by Abu Nazir. The writer wanted to put that part of Carrie's illness to work. "I was trying to figure out a way that she was seeing some big thing that we couldn't see. There is a sort of a logic or sense to it, even though it's grandiose. Her little details seem crazy, but after she has charted out everything physically that was in her mind, then we can actually see why it makes sense to her."

Saul spends the night in Carrie's apartment, organizing the papers by colored groups, indeed revealing a gap in activity, which turns out to correspond to the time Nazir was mourning Issa. "What's different about Saul is that he sees her beautiful mind. It's not nonsense," Stiehm says.

For the design of the wall, Stiehm sketched out a rough diagram; but on the day of the shoot on October 13, she still wasn't satisfied with how it would come together. "Just a couple hours before the scene was shot, [staff writer] Charlotte Stoudt and I sat at the coffee table for two hours with two prop guys, and we just started highlighting documents and circling pictures." The image, once assembled, was so striking that it became an iconic symbol of the show.

In the middle of her mania, Carrie calls Brody to ask his help regarding her find—and he immediately calls Estes, who arrives with a team to take down the wall. Both men have much to hide. "For Brody, it's a street fight," says director Clark Johnson. "You have to be prepared to win at all costs, to be brutal. She's getting too close to the truth. He thinks, 'She's vulnerable right now, and I'm gonna use that and turn it against her.'"

Estes also has no interest in Carrie revealing the truth. "The further she digs, the closer she will get to the drone strike," actor David Harewood explains. "The wall is taking her close to why Abu Nazir is attacking, and I don't want anybody to find that out. I'm under orders to bury that completely."

In a scene that likely had much to do with Claire Daines receiving an acting Emmy the following year, Carrie reacts in horror as her world is taken apart by the agents. "It's painful," says Stiehm. "She's in this state where she can't be believed, even if she's right, because she's so clearly unstable—and then she's been betrayed by Brody and Estes."

Johnson allowed the actors to improvise during shooting, with cinematographer Nelson Cragg operating his handheld camera embedded within the cast. Notes colleague Michael Cuesta, "With Claire, in a scene like that, you just let her go, and just capture it." Says Johnson, "I kept making Claire do it again and again and again, and she really did start to lose it," prompting Harewood to instinctively hug the actor during the shoot. "She was screaming and crying, and I put my arms around her, I just reacted. I found myself just standing there, watching Claire, watching this brilliance."

The scene indeed took a great deal out of the actor, writer Chip Johannessen notes. "It was a lot to ask a human being to do, to get to that place, and then do it over and over again. It's a remarkable performance."

Writer Meredith Stiehm's original concept sketch for the Rainbow Wall.

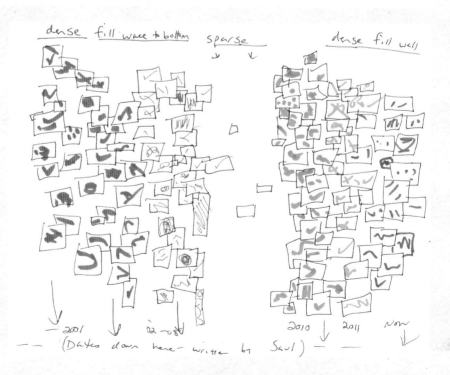

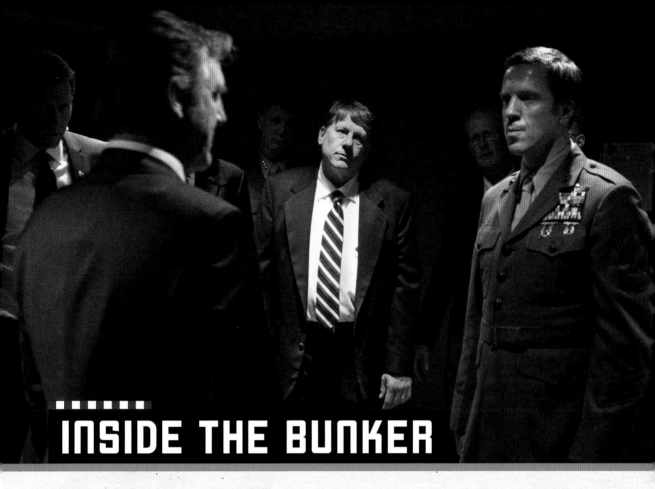

INSIDE THE BUNKER

THERE HAVE BEEN FEW MORE COMPEL-ling scenes on television than that in which Nicholas Brody is trapped inside a security bunker with the Vice President of the United States and dozens of others, deciding whether to blow them all up, as in the Season 1 finale, "Marine One."

"We always knew we were going to get Brody on the verge of committing a big terrorist act," showrunner Alex Gansa says. It then became about how it would occur and what he would do. "By midseason," says writer Chip Johannessen, "we understood that it would have something to do with getting this group of people that you could ordinarily never assemble in one place into one place. The idea that evolved was some kind of event disrupted by sniper fire, and that emergency protocols would be enacted to move people into a building and assembled in a tight place. Then it would be easy to take them out."

The episode was structured in three parts over three days. "We wanted the middle section to be like *24*, so we structured the whole episode that way," says Johannessen, who cowrote the show with Alex Gansa. The format suited direc-tor Michael Cuesta just fine. "It's eighty-five minutes long. I approached it like one of my independent films. I knew exactly how to design it and what I wanted."

Brody actually begins the first day by creat-ing a "martyr video," in which he explains, for posterity, the reasons behind his actions the next day. "The suicide vest and the martyr video are such iconic tropes, both of which we upend," says executive producer Howard Gordon. The video also offered opportunities for the future, Johannessen adds. "We thought it would be a great thing to leave behind, which could create problems next year."

The sniping scenes, where Tom Walker shoots Elizabeth Gaines and several others, were filmed with 150 extras over the weekend of October 29 and 30, on the steps of the Old Civil Courthouse in downtown Charlotte, subbing in for the State

Department in Washington. "It's beautiful architecture from the '70s, much like the real building," states production designer John Kretschmer. "We added a quote from Thomas Jefferson in the lobby, along with a WPA-type mural," painted by artist Helen Ward.

As Brody gets dressed that morning, he, most unusually, prevents Dana from entering his bedroom, lest she see the vest, part of the "living with a terrorist" concept that appealed to the writers. "She's been noticing things about her dad for weeks," says actor Morgan Saylor. "But this day, the feeling really hits. She knows something isn't right." The scene was wishful thinking on the part of several of the writers, who had teenagers at home, says Johannessen. "She knows something is wrong with her dad and cares enough to get up out of her room and ask, 'Dad, are you okay in there?' Which is a way that no teenager in history has ever behaved."

Once Brody is inside the bunker, Carrie's own instincts kick in, and she comes to the Brody house to warn Dana of her father's likely intentions. Carrie begins addressing a frightened Dana, just as her mother arrives. "This woman, who was with my husband, who is perceived to be insane, is actually trying to warn us of something that is very, very real," says Morena Baccarin. "Jessica, of course, is the lioness, and tells her, 'Get out of my house,' but it sinks in. Somewhere in her she knows Carrie's not crazy, that she's telling the truth."

The scene was an intense one to shoot for the three women. "Claire is just incredible to watch," says Baccarin. "Claire can do the same scene over and over again, and every time it still feels real."

Brody, meanwhile, finally works himself up to attempt to set off the bomb, with Cuesta capturing every moment of the incredible intensity of Lewis's performance. "I shot that with a 20mm lens, which is a super wide angle," the director explains. "The camera was only five inches from his face, and it captures and exaggerates every little facial tick. He's struggling with his decision, and the camera just picks up everything. Damian understood that choice. He could work from the inside, without having to project much."

The bomb fails and Brody retreats to the bathroom to make a repair. "He had to rip it open and fix it over several takes," says prop master Gillian Albinski. "So we had three vests we'd made, and I and our seamstress kept repairing them, so they could do as many takes as they needed."

In one of the most memorable scenes of the entire series, just as Brody is about to make a second attempt, he receives a phone call from Dana, who, having taken Carrie's message to heart, begs him to promise that he will come home. "She doesn't want to believe her dad is a terrorist," Saylor says. "But she wouldn't call if she didn't believe Carrie at all. She just wants him to come home, to be her dad."

Saylor and Lewis actually performed their sides of the conversation for their scene mate via telephone, Saylor pulling into a parking lot for two hours while driving to Charlotte, and Lewis at Charlotte Airport on his way out, both on different days. "We try to do that as much as possible on *Homeland,*" Lewis states. "If someone's there on the set, you hear them behind walls. The phone creates a real authenticity."

The idea for the scene came from a similar promise Chip Johannessen had made with his young daughter, promising her he would quit smoking. "It made it bizarrely easy for me to stop," he recalls. "I always thought, 'Who would lie to *your* four-year-old?' I think Brody is in the same place. Dana backs him into it, where he has to promise something that he does not want to promise her. But once he's done that, he's coming home. He would not lie to her."

"It's about love," says Lewis. "It's about personal, humane, corporeal love, winning over any sort of abstract ideologies or principals that one lives one's life by. It's the pure, raw fact of human relationships. And that's what brings him back from the edge."

Director Michael Cuesta explains the inner workings of a Canon video camera to Damian Lewis. Note the scaffolding behind, leading to the roof of the Brody home, for filming a scene with Morgan Saylor.

WHAT IS ECT?

After struggling through the effects of her untreated Bipolar Disorder at the end of "Marine One," Carrie finally makes the decision to receive Electro-Convulsive Therapy (ECT), formerly known as Electroshock Therapy, in order to effect some relief.

"That was Alex Gansa's idea," notes writer Chip Johannessen. "He really wanted to leave her in a messed up state at the end of the whole matter, and that was a good way to do it."

Interestingly, many patients who receive ECT, as in Carrie's case, do so voluntarily, says Dr. Jay Yeomans, Service Chief of the Electroconvulsive Therapy Department with Carolinas Healthcare. Dr. Yeomans has worked with ECT for 25 years and was brought in as a consultant for the episode. "It's recommended if the patient doesn't respond well to medication, particularly if their depression has reached a point that they're psychotic or they're a danger to themselves," he says. "People, in fact, often respond to medications after they have ECT that they didn't respond to before."

ECT has come a long way since the days of *One Flew Over the Cuckoo's Nest*, the 1975 film in which a more or less sane Jack Nicholson is given a disturbing series of shock treatments. "[Producer] Michael Klick asked me if I would serve as a technical consultant, and I said yes, but only if they would portray it accurately. He assured me that they wanted it to be authentic, which it was."

Unlike the image most people have of ECT, the apparently torturous seizures portrayed in *Cuckoo's Nest* no longer occur. "It did use to cause brain damage and memory loss years ago. But that's no longer the case. There's very minimal memory loss, if any." The patient, in fact, is completely unaware of the treatment while it is happening. Patients are given an anesthetic agent, which puts them to sleep, and then given a paralytic agent, which paralyzes the entire body, with the exception of the calf of one leg, allowing the psychiatrist to observe any seizure. "They're sound asleep," Yeomans says. "A lot of times they wake up after and say, 'Well, when are you going to do the treatment?'"

ECT acts, Yeomans explains, "like a CTRL+ALT+DELETE button on your brain. We're rebooting your brain just like you would reboot your computer. It resets the neural transmitters." The exact mechanism that occurs is, to this day, still unknown. "We have a lot of theories. But we know it works. We know it's more effective than medications."

In the procedure, conductive paddles are applied to one or both of the patient's temples. The paddles are connected to a device that delivers electrical energy. The amount of energy delivered depends on several parameters but, as a rule of thumb, begins at a lower level and is slowly increased until a physical seizure is observed in the nonparalyzed leg. "You only need to give them enough to induce a seizure, but no more than that," Yeomans explains. "They used to give everybody 100 percent energy, which was overkill, and that's why people had headaches and memory loss." Patients typically receive a course of twelve treatments, dispensed two or three times a week. Maintenance treatments are often given once or twice a year, or as frequently as needed.

For the sequence in "Marine One," Danes and director Michael Cuesta studied YouTube videos to understand how treatments take place and how the patient behaves. The scenes were filmed at the Piedmont Medical Center in Rock Hill, South Carolina, using Yeomans's own Somatics Thymatron ECT instrument. Though unplanned, Yeomans himself ended up portraying the physician delivering the treatment. "The day of the filming, they said, 'Instead of you showing somebody how to act as an ECT psychiatrist, why don't you just do it?'" Yeomans was happy to oblige.

Yeomans explained the process to Danes, making sure to show her that the stimulus paddles were absolutely not connected to the machine before he fired it up. Three passes were filmed: one realistically portraying the near absence of movement, one with some exaggerated movement, and another with a full set of *Cuckoo's Nest*–type convulsions. "I think they went with the middle one, for creative reasons," Yeomans notes.

Just before she receives the treatment, Carrie suddenly remembers one word: "Issa." "She's always operational," Johannessen says. "She's always doing her job."

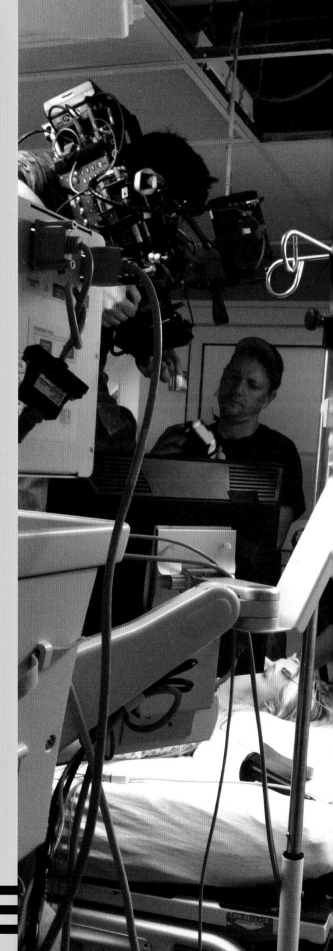

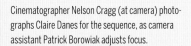
Cinematographer Nelson Cragg (at camera) photographs Claire Danes for the sequence, as camera assistant Patrick Borowiak adjusts focus.

SEASON TWO

★ *HOMELAND'S* SECOND SEASON

premiered on September 30, 2012, after great antici-
pation following the major Emmy wins for Season 1 just
two weeks before, including trophies for Outstanding
Drama Series and acting wins for Claire Danes and
Damian Lewis.

Fans, of course, wanted to know what had happened to Carrie and
Brody. Last seen receiving electroconvulsive therapy, Carrie is now enjoying a peaceful, post-CIA recovery at her sister's house, but it doesn't
last long. When a former informant in Beirut tells Saul she has some
news for the CIA but will speak only to Carrie, the former agent receives
an unwelcome invitation from an only slightly contrite David Estes to
come back and help.

Carrie's return is not an easy one, but she does what Carrie Mathison
does best: disobeys orders and gets results. Her informant alerts the
team to a forthcoming meeting involving Abu Nazir, and Nazir is almost
taken out by U.S. snipers—except there's a snag. Sgt. Brody is now
Congressman Brody, having abandoned his bunker and suicide vest for
an office and a briefcase. Vice President Walden, wanting to continue
riding the Brody popularity train, approaches Brody to recruit him as
his own running mate in the upcoming Presidential Election. Walden,
however, is not alone in the recruiting department: Abu Nazir has not
forgotten his American "helper," and Brody soon finds himself continuing
to be forced to do Nazir's bidding, under direction of a Nazir operative, a
reporter named Roya Hammad. He even quietly texts Nazir a last-minute
warning from the Joint Chiefs command center that allows Nazir to avoid
the snipers—while sitting right beside the Vice President!

Jessica is exploring her new life as a congressman's wife. At the
invitation of Mrs. Walden, she gets involved in a charity benefitting
returning veterans. Jessica asks Brody to perform the keynote speech
at a large event, but Brody misses the dinner—the congressman is busy
attempting to collect Gettysburg's infamous tailor and ends up burying
him. Jessica has to speak in his stead, a frustration that becomes the last
straw, and she forces Brody out of the house to a hotel.

Dana now attends a fancy private school, where she makes but one
new friend: the Waldens' son, Finn. A 180-degree turn from her previous
stoner beau, Xander, Finn charms Dana—until the two run over a woman
in an alley while on an evening joyride trying to outrun the Secret Service.

Saul discovers the memory card containing Brody's martyr video,
exonerating Carrie—she was right about Brody all along. Estes sets up
a new surveillance team, run by a mysterious new "analyst" named Peter
Quinn, and Carrie is ordered to reconnect with Brody, in hopes of quietly
retrieving information about Nazir. Unable to resist the opportunity, she

instead busts Brody and, shortly thereafter, interrogates him, ending (for the moment) his life of lies and getting him to agree to work on their side against Nazir, in exchange for immunity.

When the woman she and Finn injured with the car dies, Dana's conscience can no longer bear covering up their actions. At a fund-raiser at a country estate, she forces Finn to join her in confessing to their parents—thus ending her relationship with Finn. Dana is ready to face the consequences, but the Waldens announced they will "handle" the situation. They pay off the woman's daughter in exchange for silence, a decision that doesn't sit well with any member of the Brody family.

Nazir appears to be moving ahead with plans for another attack. Roya meets with a new, dangerous, unknown operative who has plans underway to explode a bomb at a military base, where the Vice President—and Brody—will be in attendance. After the operative stages an attack on the CIA while retrieving munitions from the tailor's shop in Gettysburg, Brody finally begins to crack. He's now lost everyone except Carrie—and he tells Roya to inform Nazir that he wants out. Instead he is taken away by helicopter to see Nazir, who explains his plans and makes it clear that he expects Brody's cooperation.

Upon his release by Nazir, Brody realizes his family is in danger, and the agency places them in an upscale safe house. Mike Faber, meanwhile, with prodding from fellow Marine Lauder Wakefield, has been attempting to find out more about what happened to Tom Walker, but is quickly shut down by Saul and Estes. So before long "Uncle Mike's" attentions are back on Jessica and the Brody kids, and by the end of the season, Jessica and Brody have decided to finally part ways.

Saul conducts his own private investigation of Peter Quinn and discovers that he is an assassin brought in by Estes—with the help of another seasoned agent, Dar Adal—to kill Brody after Nazir is taken out. As Saul uncovers more about Estes's and Walden's involvement in the drone attack that killed Nazir's son, Estes tries to clamp him down, detaining and interrogating Saul in an attempt to discredit him.

Nazir kidnaps Carrie and takes her to his hiding place in a derelict factory. He uses her capture as leverage to force Brody to help him assassinate the Vice President—which Brody does by sneaking the terrorist the codes that operate the Veep's pacemaker, allowing Brody to finally avenge Issa's death. Carrie escapes from Nazir and initiates a military search to find him—a search that results in Nazir's death.

While Nazir is being buried at sea, a memorial for Walden is held at the CIA. And as the event gets under way, an enormous bomb explodes, killing hundreds, including Estes. It is soon discovered that the bomb had been carried in Brody's car, and he and Carrie find themselves on the run. She supplies him with forged identification and takes him to the Canadian border to escape, then returns to join a grieving Saul, now acting director over the decimated CIA. All fingers remain pointed at Brody.

CONGRESSMAN BRODY—A FRESH START?

AFTER A SUCCESSFUL END TO SEASON 1 in mid-December, the writing team met at the Writers' Room in the *Homeland* office at Fox in late January 2012 to begin thinking about how to move the series forward. "Season 1 had gotten picked up late by the network, so we were always scrambling to catch up," informs writer Chip Johannessen. "When we went back into the room, Season 2 was just this big, gaping hole."

One of the ideas tossed around involved Iran and its nuclear program, and that ended up appearing briefly as an element of the Season 2 storyline. But the big question remained: what to do about Brody? The writers had always entertained the possibility that Brody would not survive the first season, and now they thought it was unlikely he would survive the second. They wrote two episodes to get the ball rolling, "The Smile" and "Beirut Is Back," and around the time Alex Cary began writing the third, "State of Independence," the team pitched their plan for Season 2 to Showtime.

"The idea was that the net would gradually tighten around Brody," Cary states, "with Carrie caught in that net with him. Between them, they would come to understand that Brody was a dead man, that his course was run." Brody would, at some point—unable to put a bullet in his own head—essentially beg Carrie to end his life. "There would be some scene that would appear to be romantic in its choreography, but would end up being a mercy killing/execution of Brody at Carrie's hand," perhaps by around Episode 8 or 9.

Showtime, though, had realized ("And they were probably right," Cary notes) that audiences loved the Carrie-Brody dynamic, and that doing away with it so early in the series was not what viewers would want to see. "So we then came up with the whole concept of Abu Nazir coming and pulling off a huge attack on America, but from the grave," the writer says.

"The big idea for us," says showrunner Alex Gansa, "was that at the end of Season 1, everybody thought Brody was innocent, but Carrie thought he was guilty. Here, we would completely reverse that dynamic, which is that the world would think he was guilty, but Carrie would believe he was innocent."

At the beginning of "The Smile," three months have passed since the bunker incident, and Sgt. Brody has become Congressman Brody, replacing the unseemly Dick Johnson. Brody appears to have convinced Nazir that he could effect more change by changing policy. Says Johannessen, "but whether Nazir has bought the plan or not is questionable."

Brody appears quite happy in his new life and seems to have left the world of explosive vests and terrorism behind. Then in walks Roya Hammad, a reporter who shares a "mutual friend" with the junior congressman—Abu Nazir. "We wanted Brody to feel settled in his new life, until this woman walks into his office and says, 'More is required of you,'" Johannessen notes. Such as

stealing an encryption key from Estes's office, for starters.

The imposition of Roya in Brody's life makes for great drama. Says Cary, "Having gone through the business with the vest, and it not working, he feels that he's done his bit. So then to be press-ganged into service by somebody who comes out of left field is an affront and also a cause for alarm and panic. He realizes in Season 2 how big the hole is that's been dug for him. And there's no getting out of it. It's just a question of how long he can survive."

Meanwhile, Vice President Walden presses Brody into a different kind of service—as his running mate in the Presidential race. "Walden loves a good and true solider," says actor Jamey Sheridan. "But it is also the best possible PR move. Brody and his young family work perfectly for selling the vice president for president." If only Abu Nazir didn't have other plans.

ACTION IN BEIRUT

AT THE BEGINNING OF SEASON 2, IN "The Smile," Carrie Mathison, like Brody, has a new life. She's quietly living with her sister, Maggie, and her family, and teaching English to Middle Eastern émigrés. "Carrie's had just enough time to get her foot into a really grounded, normal life," says director Michael Cuesta. But this is the world of *Homeland*. That peace can't last.

The problem for the writers lay in how to get Carrie back in the game, after the exposure of her illness and subsequent ouster from the Agency. "We had a kind of *24*-ish problem," says writer Chip Johannessen, a veteran of that series. "It was like Jack Bauer is on the outs, how do we bring him back in? So we did a *24*-type of reentry for Carrie," where an informant will talk only to Carrie, thus requiring her services in Beirut.

Though she appears resistant, it's not a tough sell. "It's like an addiction for Carrie," Cuesta states. "It's hard for her to pass up."

"She's a big junkie, in terms of her job," notes Johannessen. "She needs the action. And when she gets back in, that stable life with Maggie goes out the door."

The writers were baffled as to how to end "The Smile." Their original pass had Carrie, while being chased, making a harrowing escape by helicopter to a Zodiac boat out in the water. But, Johannessen recalls, "I said, 'She's back in it—let's do a thing where she just smiles.'" It was a welcome suggestion, Cuesta says. "You don't see Carrie smile a lot, so when she does, you just love it. And when you see it, it's like, 'I'm back. This is my bliss.' I got it in one take. And when we showed it at the New York premiere, everybody clapped when they saw her smile."

The events of the previous season have nonetheless taken their toll on Carrie. While in Beirut, she overhears Saul and Estes expressing their doubts over her stability. "She's unmoored now, in some basic way," says Johannessen. Being able to trust her gut had always carried her, but now, having been "wrong" about Brody, Carrie doesn't know what to trust.

After hearing Saul and Estes's conversation, Carrie goes to the roof of the safe house and has an anxiety attack. "It's a crisis of confidence, a near breakdown," Cuesta says. "We had shot a similar scene for the pilot, but it was too soon for the audience to see that. Now was the time."

The season's production began filming in Israel, returning in mid-May, this time working nine days, compared to the two worked the previous year. States co-executive producer Michael Klick, "In Season 1, we had two small scenes to do. Now, we had more to construct, more set pieces, and more locations." Once again, the crew had to film in crowded open markets and in traffic in cities like Tel Aviv and Jaffa. "There were people pissed about everything all the time, screaming and yelling. We had a lot to pull off."

With his wife gone, Saul has set up a new life in Beirut, working out of the American embassy there to deal with the local situation, which includes a large demonstration outside the complex. The scenes were filmed at the former mayor's mansion/town hall in Tel Aviv, now a museum. As they did during the previous year's visit, things got a little rough, Cuesta recalls. "We dressed a lot of Israeli extras as Hezbollah, with yellow scarves and headbands. I had four or five cameras going, and in the middle of the shoot, an Israeli ex-military guy saw what was happening and ran into the demonstration and started beating the hell out of one of the Hezbollah guys!" The scene was stopped, and the conflict was resolved. "Minutes later the two men were best friends, and the guy invited the extra over for tea. I guess we did a good job, it was very real."

The impulsive Carrie decides at the last minute, after retrieving her informant, to dash into

ABOVE: Stunt coordinator (white T-shirt) Cal Johnson, actor Navid Negahban (Abu Nazir) and director Michael Cuesta ready a take during the Nazir assassination sequence in Haifa.

BELOW: Director Michael Cuesta poses with Navid Negahban (Abu Nazir) and his posse of Hezbollah extras during the shoot in Haifa on May 20, 2012.

an apartment complex to collect evidence. This ends up having a profound effect, when among the materials Carrie collects is a memory card, on which Saul discovers Brody's martyr video. "That was such a Carrie move," Johannessen says. "She goes back into this 'burning building,' with guys chasing her, and barely makes it out. It looks like she hasn't gotten anything, but she's actually gotten something amazing."

Cuesta shot the scenes, with Danes doing her own running about, in a busy *shuk* (market) in the city of Jaffa, once again making use of Gideon Raff's *Hatufim* crew, as he had the previous year. "I filmed it in pieces, so Claire didn't have to run too much," the director recalls. "It's shot subjectively, with the camera very much on the operators' shoulders, following her. You're witnessing this with her, doing it with her. It was one of my favorite scenes to shoot."

The CIA's assassination attempt on Nazir was shot in Haifa, an hour north of Tel Aviv, at an older apartment complex with tall walls,

perfect for creating a sense of an ambush. "We shot it in a day. We bussed everybody up early in the morning, shot all afternoon, then drove back that night," recalls Klick.

Brody, of course, has never lost his allegiance to Nazir and, even though sitting in the Joint Chiefs Ops Room with the Vice President, secretly texts a warning to Nazir just in time to save his life. "That wasn't in the first script draft," Johannessen recalls. "Alex Gansa read my draft and said, 'Wouldn't it be cooler if Brody could somehow intervene?' That became much cooler."

The Ops Room was purposely set up to resemble the famous shot of President Obama and his Joint Chiefs during the Osama bin Laden assassination. Cuesta and crew, of course, couldn't resist the photo op and struck identical poses on set in Charlotte to those of Obama and friends.

Upon returning from filming in Israel at the beginning of June, one of the scenes production shot was a visit by Brody to a still-ailing Carrie in the hospital. The piece was shot solely for use as a Season 2 teaser clip and added to the Season 1 DVD set that was being prepared just as Season 2 was about to premiere. Similarly, a Season 3 teaser clip for the Season 2 DVD set was shot in Puerto Rico by producer Michael Klick during Season 3 work, showing Brody running through the jungle with a shotgun. It appears nowhere in any episode.

TOP: The now-famous White House Joint Chiefs photo, as President Obama watches the takedown of Osama bin Laden.

BOTTOM: The production team reenacts President Obama's Osama bin Laden Joint Chiefs pose. Front row: Assistant director Ken Collins, director Michael Cuesta, showrunner Alex Gansa, cinematographer Nelson Cragg, video playback specialist Jen Martin, editor Jordan Goldman; Back row: Camera operator Bob Newcomb, camera operator Nick Davidoff, assistant prop master Kelly Rubottom, Damian Lewis, gaffer Tommy Sullivan.

ROYA HAMMAD

"DIRECT COMMUNICATION BETWEEN Brody and Nazir was impossible," Alex Gansa explains. "So we needed a middleman between the two. And since Carrie was going to run Brody back against the Nazir network, we needed people on U.S. soil that were bad guys."

The writers eventually settled on a female news anchor. "We decided on a woman who did international stories, and could therefore travel around the globe with a degree of impunity." Adds writer Alex Cary, "We wanted a sophisticated, intelligent woman, who was as at home with the Washington, D.C., circuit as she was with a bunch of soldiers on the back of a Blackhawk in Afghanistan." Educated in the West, she also needed to have a strong proclivity against the West, as might the daughter of Palestinian refugees.

The producers cast beautiful London-born Zuleikha Robinson in the part of Roya Hammad. "I remember watching the audition," recalls director Michael Cuesta. "Mandy Patinkin was over my shoulder, saying, 'She's terrific. You're going with her, right, Michael?' I said, 'Yeah, I think I am.'"

Robinson plays the terrorist with a seething but controlled rage. "I tried to muster up as much anger as I could, and just have that underneath the surface," she relates. "She's just steely."

In Robinson's view, her character expected a warmer reception out of Brody than she received. "Given his relationship with Issa and Abu Nazir, she was quite sure that it would be a welcome response," the actress explains. "But he essentially wants to shut her down. She trusts him for the first few episodes, but as time goes on, that trust is chipped at."

"STATE OF INDEPENDENCE"

BY THE THIRD EPISODE, "STATE OF Independence" (filmed after episode four, "New Car Smell"), the pressure on Brody is beginning to take its toll. The CIA has a lead on Bassel, the Gettysburg tailor, who needs to be moved to a safe house; and Brody is the member of Nazir's network who can get to him first, as determined by his new handler, Roya Hammad. "Congressman or not, that's what he has to do," says writer Alex Cary.

But Bassel is overcome with paranoia, and, while they're on the road, he tries to escape Brody. "He thinks he's been compromised," Cary explains. "He thinks Brody has come to pick him up and dispense with him. It's like in *Goodfellas*, where the person who's going to kill you is going to claim to be your friend. That's what's going on in his little mind."

A foot chase ensues, and Bassel trips over a piece of barbed wire and impales himself with a fence post (in a scene performed by stunt double Rob Weir). Knowing the tailor will never survive,

and in a hurry to get back to Washington to keep a commitment to Jessica to speak at a fund-raiser, Brody snaps his neck and buries him there in the woods. "Brody finds himself in a weird situation, almost a combat situation, and, for the tailor's own good, kills him quickly and mercifully," says Cary. "But the caretaker of the situation is someone who's equally paranoid, confused, and panicked. It all goes wrong for him, and that's where he begins to lose his mind."

The chase scenes were filmed in various locations on open highway around Mooresville in muggy 96-degree weather around the Fourth of July. The killing of Bassel was filmed in Hornets Nest Park, near the *Homeland* production facility. "It has really great old-growth forest, perfect for this kind of scene," notes production designer John Kretschmer. Gear had to be carried in and out by hand. "It actually took a lot of planning, by us and by our stunt coordinator," with an effects rig with a fake fence post, a rubber rock (for Bassel to hit Brody on the head with) and, as the July 5 call sheet states, "Lots o' blood."

For a quick cleanup (so nobody will notice), Brody runs himself through a self-service car wash, sans car. The scene was filmed at a car wash around the corner from the studio, rigged with a low-pressure sprayer "so he wouldn't blast himself too hard, as would have happened with the real car wash hose," notes producer Michael Klick.

"We had him washing himself in a car wash, which is insane," states Cary. "It begs the question for anyone driving by, 'What the fuck is going on there?'" Even while shooting at the location, Cary wondered if it was too outlandish. "I discussed it with Damian, and he said, 'Yeah, he would probably do it.'" Lewis adds, "He's so damaged, he becomes irrational."

Brody doesn't get back to town in time to deliver his speech at the fund-raiser for veterans. In his absence, Jessica is forced to make the speech herself. "I was immediately intimidated by it," upon reading the script, laughs actress Morena Baccarin. "She did a great job," says director Michael Cuesta. "It's a challenge to not overplay something like that. If the scene is a speech, an actor has to make those words be fully truthful, like they're their own."

Baccarin had two things going for her. "When Alex wrote that speech, it obviously came from somewhere very real in him, and I wanted to do it justice," she says. It also helped that the downtown Charlotte Ritz-Carlton's Ballroom, where the scene was filmed, was filled with more than 200 extras, many of them actual war veterans, including a number of amputees, in their own uniforms. "When I got up on that stage to shoot that scene, I was really drawn in by them, and it just came out of me the way you see it." Her delivery had a powerful effect, says Kretschmer. "It was really gratifying to be on set that day and watch her pull that out and find her moment." Adds Cary,

"I think that was her finest moment in the show, actually."

Jessica's husband's absence at the fund-raiser doesn't go unnoticed, says actor Marc Menchaca, reprising the disabled veteran Lauder Wakefield. "I had one line in that episode: 'Fucking Brody.'"

Director Lodge Kerrigan discusses a shot with Damian Lewis. It was Kerrigan's film, *Keane*, starring Lewis, which first attracted *Homeland*'s producers to their star

DANA AND FINN

WITH THE BRODYS' FOCUS HAVING shifted from "Is Dad a terrorist?" to "Dad's a congressman," Dana's life has changed, and part of it is not to her liking. She now attends an upscale Quaker school, the Colton School, and as Morgan Saylor says, "It's not her cup of tea. She doesn't share a lot of beliefs with many of the people there."

The writers modeled Colton after schools like Washington's Holton-Arms and National Cathedral schools in order to place Dana in a world that was clearly not her own. "We wanted to give her a new environment," says writer Meredith Stiehm. "I spent eighth grade at National Cathedral School. She's experiencing the experience I had with those kinds of teenagers."

Production designer John Kretschmer also had some experience with Quaker schools, his daughters having spent their middle school years in one. "A Quaker school typically has a plain and simple look, which is part of the

Quaker culture, but we went with a visually more interesting choice." The look of Colton was created from a myriad of interiors cobbled together from different locations. Queens University in Charlotte was used for exteriors, such as when Brody drops Dana off for class, and many interiors were shot at Cornwell Center's Myers Park Baptist Church.

The Quaker "town meeting," in which Dana lets slip that her father is a Muslim, was filmed at Winthrop University, across the state border in Rock Hill, South Carolina. It is there that she meets a dashing young man, Finn Walden, who happens to be the Vice President's son, played by Timothée (French, pronounced tee-mo-TAY) Chalamet. The actor, who was unfamiliar with *Homeland* at the time he auditioned, was told that his character was a prep boy and snobby. "Living in New York," Chalamet says, "I definitely know who that kid is."

A far cry from her old flame, Xander, Finn has almost immediate appeal for Dana. "Finn is charming, certainly not a word that could be used to describe Xander," Saylor says. Adds director Michael Cuesta, "We portrayed Xander as a rudderless stoner dude. Dana's impressed with Finn's wit, but she's also drawn to the goodness in him." Chalamet says, "She likes the arrogant confidence he has, and the incredible steadiness that he projects." As for Dana's appeal for Finn, Chalamet notes, "He likes that she's different. The first day in school, she interrupts a class assembly and does her own thing. She became a misfit at her school almost on impact. So he thought, 'Hey, maybe if I can make this girl my girlfriend, people will really think that's awesome,' dating the girl that nobody knows. They come from different worlds, and, as they say, opposites attract."

Finn suffers from the heavy burdens his bullying father has placed on him, a story element writer Henry Bromell championed. "It's a world where, on a superficial level, it seems like an easy and privileged life," Chalamet explains. "But growing up the son of a Vice President, Finn has an unrealistic amount of expectation put on him." Adds Stiehm, "He's really terrified of his dad. He wants to be close to him, wants his dad to be proud of him, but he doesn't know how to talk to his father." This is a sentiment echoed by Jamey Sheridan, who plays the VP.

Sheridan notes, however, "Walden doesn't think of himself as a bully. He's probably only spent four hours with his son in the last three years. And he definitely doesn't know how to talk to his son. He's the kind of guy who tells his teenage boy an off-color, grown-up joke, and expects him to get it, and then asks, 'What's the matter with you?'"

Walden's idea of "toying" with his son amounts to insulting him and belittling him, something that doesn't go unnoticed by Dana when she and Finn are studying at the Vice President's Mansion at the Naval Observatory (actually Charlotte's Duke Mansion). "She can see he's not good to his son, and she likes his son," says Stiehm. Dana throws a pointed jab at the Vice President, regarding the unearned "Gentleman's Cs" (passing grades given to an underachieving student of an influential family) that she infers Walden received in his own past. "He gets some of his own medicine," concedes Sheridan. "She talks to him the way he talks to Finn."

Finn and Dana go on a first date to the top of the Washington Monument (filmed at a replica built onstage at the *Homeland* stages, and the scene features what was, for both actors, their first onscreen kiss. "It was weird meeting him the first time, knowing ahead of time I'd be kissing him," Saylor recalls. Chalamet says, "It was nerve-racking, with thirty people standing around watching, not to mention knowing that your high school friends are going to see it.

Man, you gotta make sure you know what you're doing up there," he laughs. The two actors have remained friends, and, to this day, Saylor kids Chalamet about his nervousness. "I tell her, 'No, I wasn't nervous. Leave me alone.'"

The young couple's second date isn't as much fun. On a spontaneous joyride, Finn accidentally strikes a woman in an alley. The woman eventually dies from her injuries. The scene was filmed over two nights in downtown Charlotte. The first night, production shot the couple on a "process trailer" (a car placed on a special vehicle, which is towed by a truck, with cameras situated alongside them). On the second night a stunt team performed the actual hit.

Chalamet unintentionally provided the only levity in the situation. Being a kid from New York, even at sixteen, he had not yet had a need to learn how to drive. "The morning of the Washington Monument scene, they had a female teamster give me a crash course in driving a BMW," he recalls. "It was nerve-racking. I didn't want to hit the wrong pedal and run over the entire crew!"

ABOVE: Camera operator Nick Davidoff films a scene with Timothée Chalamet and Morgan Saylor outside Queens University in Charlotte.

When it came time to shoot his and Dana's reaction to having struck the woman, the inexperienced driver gave . . . the wrong reaction. "They were in the car on the process trailer, and I was verbally talking them through each beat, so they'd have something to respond to," recalls director Lesli Linka Glatter. Upon hearing "Now!" Chalamet threw his hands in the air

and exclaimed, "Oh, my God, oh my God!" But the car was still moving—a situation that in real life would have sent the car into a wild turn. "I had gotten myself so psyched and knew I was gonna nail it," the actor recalls. "Then I heard 'Cut' and a bunch of extremely hard laughter coming over the walkie-talkie."

Dana, of course, wants to do the right thing and call the police, but Finn will have no part of it. "There's no way anybody could find out about this," Chalamet explains. "My dad gets on my case when I get a B in school, and I work hard for that. What would he say about my taking a joyride through D.C., purposely losing the Secret Service, and then hitting a woman, who later died? For Finn, that's a lot more stressful than being caught by the police."

Finn is used to a life of privilege, one in which he knows his parents will use their influence to clean up his mess. "That was one of the goals of the scenario," says showrunner Alex Gansa, "to demonstrate how rules operate differently for different classes of people." Dana comes from a mind set where there's a morality involved, but there's no issue of morality for Finn because he wasn't brought up in a moral household. "He kills someone via illegal driving but is aware he'll get away with it," says Chalamet. "Like Paris in the *Iliad*, he's a privileged kid that is just a coward to his core."

"Dana can't eat or sleep," says Saylor. "It's eating away at her, and she wants to resolve it, not just for herself, but for this woman and her family." She goes to see the dying woman in the hospital and meets her daughter, Inez, and eventually forces Finn to join her in telling their parents of the event. "Dana's always willing to go out on a limb to make things right," says Saylor. "I was always excited to play those scenes."

The Waldens eventually pay off Inez to keep quiet about her mother's death, as Dana learns when she visits the understandably angry young woman at her home. Dana comes home and cries on her mother's shoulder. "Morena and I were good friends at that point," Saylor recalls. "It was a good cry, and a real one."

PETER QUINN

AS EPISODE 4 WAS BEING WRITTEN, THE writers still entertained the idea that Brody would be killed off sometime during the season. So a character was needed who would eventually perform that act, which led to the creation of Peter Quinn.

Saul pitches to David Estes the idea of creating an operation, headed by Carrie, to run Brody back against Nazir. "But she's not the most trustworthy person in Estes's eyes," says showrunner Alex Gansa. "So Estes needed someone else to run that operation. The question then became, who do we bring into that environment that's going to be compelling and create some new dynamic with Carrie?"

The answer was Peter Quinn, a dark ops agent, apparently brought in as an "analyst," but who has an ulterior motive. "Quinn comes in under the guise of helping Carrie out," notes writer Chip Johannessen. "But he's basically an assassin."

Director Michael Cuesta had originally considered actor Rupert Friend when casting the lead role of Sherlock Holmes for the pilot

for CBS's *Elementary* in the spring of 2012. "He would have been an edgier, darker Sherlock," Cuesta recalls. The director was taken with the actor and told the casting director, "Sorry, but I'm gonna have to cast this guy in *Homeland*," which would film just a few months later.

The Irish-born Friend was doing a Dennis Potter play, *Brimstone and Treacle*, in London, portraying a man who thinks he is the devil, when he was asked to audition for *Homeland*.

"I was building my house and had run out of money," the actor recalls. Friend recorded video auditions, with various people standing in for Claire Danes (including his sister), propping a camera up in his unfinished kitchen. "They had no script, I had nothing to read," he says. Regardless, he projected what the producers were looking for.

"He brought an anonymous feel to Quinn," states writer Meredith Stiehm. "He's compelling because you just can't place him." Adds Johannessen, "Rupert doesn't have the face of a scary guy. We wanted to cast a guy who could pass in the real world, without you going, 'Oh, there's an assassin.' You think the opposite."

One of the key parts of Quinn's personality is an absence of social grace of any kind. Not long after meeting Carrie, referring to Brody, he blurts out, "You were fuckin' him, huh?" "He doesn't have great social skills or know how to relate to people on an emotional human level," Cuesta explains. "But that became a way of discovering him."

"My favorite line," says Stiehm, "is her response to the 'fucked Brody' question: she says, 'Oh, who did you fuck last night?' and he answers, 'An ER nurse, but I'm not that into her.'" Notes Friend, "Through all that backchat and squabbling is a base of very deep mutual respect. They can smell the deep and layered intelligence in one another. Neither takes bull-shit from anybody, and I think that links them together in a certain way."

Quinn leads a sparse life, as becomes evident in the Quinn-centric episode "Two Hats," written by Alex Cary, in which Saul, Virgil, and Max explore his life. "This is a man who has sacrificed almost everything in service to his profession," says Gansa, including a girlfriend and child.

Drawing on his own military experience, Cary says, "There are but a few luxuries in that world: clean socks, cigarettes, and a good book," in Quinn's case, a copy of *Great Expectations*. "I wanted *The Old Man and the Sea*, but it would have cost too much to clear the rights." Regardless, Friend found the book a good fit for Quinn. "It was also an interesting coincidence, because my childhood nickname was 'Pip,' and that's the main character in that book," the actor says.

At the end of "Two Hats," Quinn is just about to pull the trigger on Brody, when Estes calls him off at the last second. "He is a law-abiding guy," Friend observes, "and his law is not the same as ours. His law comes from a very quiet, secret place, but it's still his law, and he follows it to the letter. If an order changes at the last minute, it changes at the last minute."

IN EPISODE 3, "State of Independence," Carrie goes from feeling worthless enough to end her life to—upon being shown Brody's martyr video by Saul—feeling completely vindicated. By the end of the following episode, she has finally busted Brody, who now has a few questions to answer.

"We knew from the beginning of the season we would have an episode, likely somewhere in the middle, that was just a long interrogation, just the two of them in a room," recalls writer Chip Johannessen. "What exactly it would look like, what the logic would be, remained to be seen." Such a story would no doubt be an important one, showrunner Alex Gansa says. "That episode would either make or break the season; we all knew it. So we had to figure out a construct that felt believable and emotional, and that ultimately resulted with Brody confessing to Carrie exactly who he was."

In the finished episode, Quinn takes a first pass at interrogating Brody, before Carrie gets her turn. But, interestingly, in writer Henry Bromell's initial drafts, Quinn was not involved at all. "There were three or four scenes, culminating in that one big twenty-minute scene between Carrie and Brody," Gansa explains. But the more the interrogation was discussed, the more Gansa felt a change was required.

"My feeling was that once Carrie got into the room with Brody, she should start and bring it on home. And if you had a bunch of scenes before that, in which she was barking up the wrong tree, you would lessen the impact of the moment when she walks into the room and begins to confess her love for Brody. So we restructured the story halfway through the writing process to have Peter Quinn insist that he's the one who has the first bite at the Brody apple."

Quinn gives it a wholehearted try, starting by playing Brody's martyr video. The scene was filmed on Rupert Friend's third day of work on *Homeland,* just after he'd joined the cast. "I missed my alarm," he recalls of that morning.

"I hadn't met Damian, I hadn't met anyone really." He and Lewis both found the situation amusing. "There we were, these two Brits, pretending to be Americans, in a dusty basement made of wood pretending to be stone, sitting in Charlotte, pretending we were in Washington," he laughs.

Brody responds by playing his usual hand, which has worked thus far: Carrie is crazy and obsessed, it's all nonsense, he doesn't know Nazir, doesn't know Issa. But the Brody shackled to the table is very different from the confidant "man in the vest" of the previous season. "Brody is a guy who was interrogated for eight years. He knows how to hold out," says director Lesli Linka Glatter. But after seeing the video, he becomes a nervous, caged animal. "He's been taken again and put in another hole, in a way. It's horrifyingly familiar."

Eventually, Quinn realizes he's hit a brick wall with Brody. "Hence the need to take drastic alternative measures," Friend comments. Adds Glatter, "He has to try a bold move to change the chess board, because the last couple of moves he thought he had Brody in checkmate, and it didn't work." Without warning, Quinn pulls a switchblade from his pocket and slams the blade through Brody's hand, pinning it to the table. He is hustled out of the room by his colleagues. "He engineers this 'good cop/bad cop' setup, which opens the door for Carrie to come in," says Gansa.

The knife gag was discussed, and Glatter and property master Gillian Albinski tried to determine the most appropriate method to create it. They eventually opted to film the move live in camera, rather than creating as a visual effect. Glatter was used to doing such shots digitally on shows like *True Blood*, but she says, "*Homeland* is not an effects show that way. So it was a matter of how to have it come out and feel fresh, unexpected, and terrifying."

The solution was found in a fake arm and hand for Damian Lewis, into which Friend would stab the knife. Makeup effects specialist John Bayless made a cast of Lewis's arm and hand, built a rubber version of the hand, and

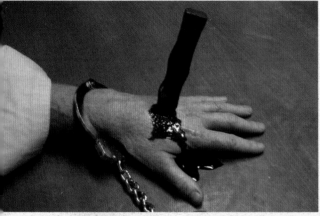

TOP: Give 'em a hand: The lifelike copy of Brody's hand on set with Quinn's knife embedded.

CENTER: Lewis's hand with a balsa wood handle glued to his skin.

BOTTOM: "How's this?" Damian Lewis tries out the finished product.

OPPOSITE: Production call sheet for July 17, 2012, indicating a number of scenes combined to film as one continuous scene. Note description, "Carrie plays good cop and convinces Brody to come clean."

painted it to look startlingly real. The construction department built a tabletop with a hole in it, to allow the knife to penetrate the rubber hand. After several test runs, Friend was filmed stabbing the rubber hand. Then the rubber arm was removed, and a lightweight balsa wood version of the knife was glued to Lewis's own hand.

A former EMT, prop master Gillian Albinski provided guidance to make sure the knife was slammed into Brody's hand in a way that would miss all the bones, muscles, and nerves. "We had a conversation about that," she says. "In real life, he'd require some serious surgery . . ."

To get in the mood, Friend kept an unseen box cutter of his own in his pocket during filming. "It made it feel more dangerous," he says. "I didn't tell Damian."

Quinn's plan works, and Carrie enters the room to begin the final interrogation. "Carrie is the best weapon against a liar like Brody," Friend notes.

Bromell's script for the scene totaled close to thirty pages. "I panicked when I first got that script," laughs Glatter. "That's a lot to shoot in one room. As a director, you have nothing to hide behind—there's no fancy camera moves you can do. It's all in in the storytelling; it either works or it doesn't. And, of course, this was brilliant."

Though Carrie's interrogation was written as a series of individual scenes and would be intercut with other footage, Glatter decided to take a chance and shoot the entire collection as one big scene, almost like a play. "Damian and Claire and Henry and I talked about what would be the best way to shoot this. Because in some ways, it was a continuous scene."

Filmed on July 17, the fifth day of production for the episode, the first take lasted twenty-five minutes, a length unheard of in television or in film. "It was chilling," Glatter recalls. During the second take, from which most of the footage was drawn, she says, "I literally felt Henry Bromell's hand reach over and grab my arm. We just stood there. I've never experienced anything like it."

Chip Johannessen, who was prepping the next episode, brought his daughter to observe the filming of the scene. "We were looking at colleges, and I rushed back to Charlotte with her, because I really wanted her to see that I just knew it was going to be an extraordinary thing."

"It was really good fun," says Damian Lewis. "Long scenes, long takes, are like being in the theater, which I enjoy. It feels like it plays out in real time."

Carrie makes use of the skills she has learned from Saul over the years, sharing her personal feelings and experience, with a sprinkling of manipulation. "Henry and Alex say that that's the way real CIA agents operate—ninety-five percent truth and five percent not," Glatter says. "Most of what Carrie is saying is absolutely true. She starts off on a personal level, and is using the relationship."

"Brody's resistant at first," Lewis notes, "and he denies knowledge, but he is slowly broken down. Carrie and Brody have a professional guise, and also an intimate connection with one another. And she succeeds in getting him to acknowledge a truth he had been protecting."

The exhausted Brody finally agrees to cooperate. "They've found him out," says Lewis. "But what's driving him is that he doesn't want any shame on himself, on his family, or on the Marine Corps. He doesn't want to be seen as an enemy of the state of America—because he remains an American. But he's damaged, he's deluded. But he's started to see, slowly, that maybe when he was sent back to America by Nazir, it looked like a good idea at the time, but he's starting to question himself. And at that moment, he becomes putty in other people's hands. He becomes malleable, and easily manipulated, because he's unclear of his own mind anymore."

The episode won a posthumous writing Emmy for Bromell, a directing nomination for Glatter, and no doubt contributed to acting nominations for Danes and Lewis, for which Danes took home a trophy. Says Johannessen, "It was the best episode of television any of us had seen in twenty years." Glatter adds, "It was one of the most profound days I've ever had on a set."

EPISODE 205 "Q & A"	fox21. HOMELAND	DATE: Tuesday July 17, 2012 DAY: of 8

DIRECTOR: Leslie Linka Glatter

CREW CALL
8:30A

PRIVATE REHEARSAL SC. 538-548 @ 7:45A

SHOOTING CALL
9:30A

EXEC. PRODUCER:	Alex Gansa
EXEC. PRODUCER	Howard Gordon
EXEC. PRODUCER	Gideon Raff
EXEC. PRODUCER	Michael Cuesta
PRODUCER:	Michael Klick
UPM:	David Brightbill
WRITTEN BY:	Henry Bromell

On-Set Production Cell: 215-___-__21 (Robert)
On-Set Locations Cell: 717-51___-__57 (Mike)

PRODUCTION OFFICE:
Bldg K

(704) ___ ___ (704)___ ___ F

SETS ARE CLOSED
No Admittance without prior approval

WEATHER: Partly Cloudy
Low: 72 High: 92 Sunrise/Sunset: 6:22A/8:37P

SET/SCENE DESCRIPTION	SCENES	CAST	D/N	PGS	
SCENES 538/339V/540/541.2/542/543.2/544/546/548 WILL BE SHOT AS ONE SCENE					Homeland Stage 2
Int. Office Space - Interrogation Brody Broke Carrie's heart. Lied to Estes. Water, please. Carrie turns off the cameras.	538,539V, 540,541.2	1, 2	D2	3 7/8	
Int. Office Space - Interrogation Carrie plays good cop and convinces Brody to come clean.	542,543.2, 544,546, 548	1, 2, 4	D2	7 6/8	DEPT HEAD STRATEGY MEETING THURS/FRI WORK: Dir/DP/Prod/ Cam/G & E/Sound/ Props/Loc/Transpo 2nd half of lunch in conf. room
***IF TIME PERMITS, MOVE TO STAGE 1 ***					
Int. Brody House - Kitchen Jess and the kids eat pizza. Brody calls.	549.1	3, 6k, 7k	N2	1 2/8	
				PAGE TOTAL 12	

NO FORCED CALLS W/O PRIOR APPROVAL FROM UPM ** NO CALL TIMES MAY CHANGE W/O A.D. APPROVAL

	CAST	CHARACTER	STATUS	PU/RPT	REHEARSAL	H/M/W	RDY	COMMENTS
1	CLAIRE DANES	CARRIE MATHISON	W	6:45A Rpt	7:45A	6:45A	9:15A	Report
2	DAMIAN LEWIS	NICHOLAS BRODY	W	CPU 7A	7:45A	7:30A	9:15A	CPU from home
3	MORENA BACCARIN	JESSICA BRODY	W	W/N @ 12 Noon				Report
4	MANDY PATINKIN	SAUL BERENSON	W	7:45A Rpt	After HMU	7:45A	8:20A	Report
5	DAVID HAREWOOD	DAVID ESTES	H	HOLD				
6k	MORGAN SAYLOR (k)	DANA BRODY	W	W/N @ 12 Noon				Report

AILEEN MORGAN

THERE ARE FEW MORE INTRIGUING supporting characters on *Homeland* than Aileen Morgan, the American terrorist who Saul skillfully interrogated during a road trip in "The Weekend." He turns to her once again in Season 2's "The Clearing," but the results aren't quite as rewarding.

Of originally casting the role for Season 1's "Clean Skin," casting director Judy Henderson recalls, "We wanted someone who could believably feel as though she was brought up in another place and came from an upper-middle-class family and rebelled against it." Henderson remembered Tony-nominated actress Marin Ireland from several Broadway plays, some of which she herself had cast. "It was difficult, because we were casting a terrorist, but Alex Gansa didn't want someone whom the audience wouldn't like. That would be too easy."

Like many aspects of the making of *Homeland*, the part of Aileen was shrouded in secrecy. "It was a minute and a half audition, and I didn't even know what was going on in the story," Ireland recalls. "Later, my agent said, 'I think you might be a terrorist.'"

Ireland and costar Omid Abtahi, who played Aileen's boyfriend, Raqim Faisel, knew little about their characters at the time they appeared together, standing outside their new house at the end of that first episode. "It's funny, because we only knew as much as the audience knew," Ireland says, noting that it wasn't until Episode 6 that she found out that Aileen indeed was the terrorist in the couple, not Faisel. "And that's really the way of the show. Aileen and Raqim were told by Abu Nazir only as much as they needed to know, as well."

Aileen would like to think of herself as stronger than she really is, the actress explains. "She likes to think of herself as 'the good soldier.' She's really trying to be as professional as possible at all times, but it's not something she's qualified for." Aileen sees her love for Raqim as a weakness. "She has the conflict of wanting to achieve her mission, and knowing her love for him is a liability. She thinks of herself as somebody who used her aloneness as a strength." Raqim's death leaves Aileen shaken. "She didn't realize how deep her love for him was, until he was gone. The feelings it leaves her with are scary and disorienting," says Ireland, "and something I don't think she saw coming."

And something Saul skillfully uses to gently break her.

When Saul returns to seek Aileen's help in "The Clearing," he finds a very different Aileen who has suffered the effects of being jailed in solitary confinement. "She's just a shell of a person, living in an altered state. She's like an animal now, completely reduced down to responding to the most essential, simple stimuli, like light and dark," says Ireland.

Saul arrives with "contraband," a few small treats, including some cheap wine. "He reminds her that she's a human, the way he did in 'The Weekend.' He reminds her that she has a heart and is a girl. And that's dangerous to do for her, because she's kind of destroyed at that point."

The actress was able to draw on her experiences of a few years earlier, when she was performing Greek plays for soldiers at military bases as part of a group called Theater of War. "We performed these scenes for guards at the detention center," she says, "and I got a glimpse into the worst of the worst of what happens, and what people do to each other. Parts of the detainees get destroyed. It's very palpable. It helped me to have witnessed that, especially when understanding what Aileen has gone through."

Saul asks for information on an accomplice of Roya Hammad's, but Aileen tells him she will provide it only if Saul is able to get her out of solitary confinement and into a cell that has a window to the outside world. When Saul leaves the visiting room to make the arrangements, Aileen takes the opportunity to break the reading glasses Saul has left on the table and slit her wrists. "Once she got out of that cell," says Ireland, "she was never going back."

Director John Dahl (holding paper) and dolly grip Michael Bonsignore watch as Mandy Patinkin and Marin Ireland rehearse a scene for "The Clearing."

DAR ADAL

WITH THE INTRODUCTION OF PETER Quinn, there had to be someone to whom he must answer. That person was Dar Adal. "He became a way to reveal what Quinn was about," explains writer Chip Johannessen.

Adal is introduced in a fleeting instance on a bus in writer Alex Cary's "Two Hats." Cary says, "We wanted to have a guy from the Dark Ops world. He represented another aspect to the CIA in the show, someone who would be working at cross purposes to Saul, not necessarily in union with him." Adal is clearly on the opposite side of the ideological side of the fence from Saul, showrunner Alex Gansa points out. "Dar Adal is somebody who got his hands dirty in the operational side of things, while Saul was focused on intelligence gathering. We liked the dichotomy between these two old men, the old lions of the agency."

Also intriguing was the concept that Adal was a CIA higher-up who was a Muslim. "The head of the Counterterrorism Unit at the real CIA, for a period of years, was a Muslim," Gansa adds. "And we just loved that idea."

Not much is known about Dar Adal—and that's on purpose. "That really should be no one's business," states F. Murray Abraham, who plays the Dark Ops chief. The actor, though, has his own thoughts: "He's a dangerous man. He's really amoral. But I think he's absolutely loyal. He'll go to the wall for this country." Abraham considers that Adal hails from a large Arab contingency that can be found in Queens. "It's his sense of loyalty that makes him so dangerous. He's been in some life and death situations, and he survived. He lives on secrets—that's part of his power. He's capable and a man to be respected and feared."

His relationship with Saul is as old as . . . Abraham's is with Mandy Patinkin. "Mandy's an old, old friend, from the theater," Abraham relates. Notes director Guy Ferland, "It was so cool to just watch these two, between shots, sit on their stools and tell stories, catch up."

Casting the role entailed finding an actor who could go toe-to-toe with someone of Patinkin's stature and experience. "That required somebody of weight and mystery and power," says Gansa, "and F. Murray kept coming up. It was fascinating to see the gamesmanship between the actors, because it completely paralleled that between the characters they were playing."

The two are first seen together at Walter's Waffles—actually the Circle G Restaurant, an old haunt of production designer John Kretschmer's growing up. "That's where my dad would go, when he'd have breakfast with the boys, way back when," he recalls—noting the "Great food, no yolk!" menu slogan was borrowed from a waffle shop at his alma mater, the University of North Carolina. Berta, the waitress seen serving Adal his usual plain waffle, is Vikki Lewis, the production's own craft service person.

Saul has come to ask Adal about the nature of Quinn's presence on his team, and the long history of their relationship is evident in Adal's response. "They're friends, but they're also professionals," Abraham explains. "He comes to me because he knows he can get a straight answer." Adal isn't afraid to speak his mind. He says to his friend, "Still afraid to get your hands dirty, Saul?" "It's a telling line," says Abraham. "I have contempt for him for not committing himself to that kind of thing. He likes giving those dirty tasks to me."

In the third season, Abraham notes, Adal begins to show his ambition and flex his muscles. But he also wants to advise Saul. "He's been around longer than Saul has, so Saul respects his judgment, even though he doesn't follow it all the time. And Adal comes from a very dark place. He lets Saul know there are certain alternatives that he's not willing to consider, by drawing on those dark experiences. They're alternatives Saul has to consider."

The name Dar Adal is fictitious, and generated, in part, as a poke from Alex Cary at his writing colleague, Henry Bromell. "Henry never got names of characters right," Cary laughs. "He'd get them slightly wrong. I was writing the episode where Adal is introduced, and Henry was writing the episode that was to follow it. Rather than call the character John Wilson or something more obviously provisional, I called him Dar Adal, just to fuck with Henry. I knew he'd never be able to get it right."

"'Dar,' in Arabic, means 'home,'" Abraham explains. "I thought that was kind of interesting—because 'home' is part of the title of this show."

THE END OF THE BRODYS

AFTER HIS RELEASE BY NAZIR, Brody asks the CIA to take measures to protect his family. The Brodys are put up in a safe house—an upscale Washington penthouse—and there Jessica makes a final decision about her relationship with her husband.

Just as she tries to begin a conversation with her husband, his cell phone rings—and guess who's calling: Carrie. "In many ways, that moment is the breakup moment," says Morena Baccarin, "because it solidifies everything. They try to have a conversation, and he still can't. And I think she just gives up."

They eventually both surrender to the inevitable and have one of their most memorable scenes, talking in the car in their driveway, the way they likely did in the early days of their relationship in high school. "You see all of their history, in a way," remarks director Jeremy Podeswa. Says Baccarin, "She's not angry with him, and she's not trying to get anything from him."

Brody begins to move toward spilling the entire truth about himself but Jessica stops him. "She tells him, 'I don't want to know.' Like, 'It's done. I just don't care anymore.' I think that release is what he's been looking for. And it's what she was afraid of." For Jessica, even if she knew the truth, the time to rebuild has passed. "I don't think it's that she would never have wanted to know," says writer Chip Johannessen. "It's just too late now. That truth is for somebody else. She senses that Carrie knows and still accepts him anyway. She says, 'Carrie must love you a lot.' What she's saying is, 'I can't deal with this shit.' And that really draws a line between them."

"The broken promises, the lack of sexual or emotional connection between these two," says showrunner Alex Gansa, "is what made their relationship bankrupt from almost the moment he got home. And I think that Jessica gave it all she had, and ultimately, she didn't have enough to give. No one would have."

NO LONGER A THREAT

ABU NAZIR IS DEAD, the threat is gone. So why kill off Brody? Peter Quinn is wondering the same thing.

"Estes is concerned Brody knows too much," says actor David Harewood. "He knows a hell of a lot about the inner workings of the CIA.

Brody and Carrie are now free to be together, and they've returned to the cabin (the same cabin they visited together in "The Weekend"). "They finally can be completely real with each other," says director Michael Cuesta.

Quinn is watching the pair from a distance, and his gears begin to turn. "Quinn is a weapon in the war on terror," says actor Rupert Friend. "His job is about removing a dangerous terrorist putting American lives at risk. Saving face for one individual, that's not Quinn's job."

As Quinn observes the loving couple, he sees the life he gave up with his girlfriend, Julia, to pursue his work. "We actually had a scene, which I cut, where he calls Julia to tell her he misses her," informs Cuesta. Instead, we see the lone

assassin, eating a can of tuna. "That's something I do," laughs writer Alex Cary. "I walk around the office with a can of tuna, which has been the source of much joking."

Quinn makes an important decision. "He sees the humanity in Carrie and Brody," says Friend. "He gave up Julia to follow his career, and he's wondering if he made the right choice. Maybe he can atone by not pulling the trigger."

His decision made, Quinn pays an unscheduled visit to Estes's bedroom, surprising him in the dark, telling him, "I'm a guy who kills bad guys." In this way he makes it clear that any more threats on Carrie and Brody will prompt a second, more deadly visit.

The scene was filmed on Harewood's emotional last day of work on the series, October 30. Harewood notes, "It's a classic spy scene. And Estes backs down. I kept wanting him to be strong, but he's weak. He always tries to project strength, but underneath, he's always been the most insecure guy in the room."

DEATH TO TYRANTS

ONCE THE WRITERS DECIDED THAT Brody would survive Season 2, they had to come up with a new battle plan. "I think we were writing Episode 8 or 9, and we didn't have the end game yet," showrunner Alex Gansa recalls.

After many frustrating story meetings, a story finally began to emerge. "We had decided that Carrie was going to be taken by Nazir, that Brody was going to be instrumental in freeing her, and that he would actually go through with his initial plan of killing Vice President Walden, with Nazir's help," explains Gansa. "Then the question became, how were we going to bring all this home?"

Walden's death would prove the key. "If Walden was killed," says Gansa, "there would be a memorial service. And if there was a memorial service, most of the people responsible for Issa's death would be there. It became clear that this would be the perfect venue for another attack." But how would a bomb make its way to the CIA? "Brody, now exonerated, would be the perfect person to get a bomb inside that compound."

The first step was to get Brody involved. So in "I'll Fly Away," Brody is kidnapped and brought to an industrial compound where Nazir is hiding. "Nazir needs a disguise," says actor Navid Negahban. "He needs to look more west-ern to enter the country," so now he's sans beard.

Nazir's relationship with Brody, however, has changed. "Our thought was that once Brody failed in his mission with the vest, Abu Nazir was, 'Never trust him again,'" explains Chip Johannessen. "So now that there is this thing that has to be done, Nazir is going to have to do it himself." Adds Negahban, "Abu is disap-pointed in Nicholas. At this point, he doesn't have time for games. If Brody doesn't get it done, Nazir will make him get it done."

Brody needs to be coerced—and that means using Carrie. Nazir kidnaps Carrie, and brings her to his hiding place (the fictional Dalton's Mill), and a complex series of scenes ensues, involving her captivity, escape, and a chase to the death for Nazir. The story spans two episodes, "Broken Hearts" (Episode 10) and "In Memoriam" (Episode 11), helmed by two different directors, Guy Ferland and Jeremy Podeswa, respectively. The episodes were filmed in two different industrial locations that are made to appear as one. It was a complex matter, to say the least. (By the way, "In Memoriam" was originally titled by Johannessen "The Motherfucker with the Turban," an homage, he says, to the 2011 Stephen Adly Guirgis play, *The Motherfucker with the Hat*. "It would have had the asterisks in there," he says, to help obscure the naughty part. The title was changed just prior to broadcast.)

The two episodes were actually filmed in reverse order. Podeswa's was shot first, while additional work on the "Broken Hearts'" script took place. It was therefore up to Podeswa, along with production designer John Kretschmer and producer Michael Klick, to find a location that would suit the storytelling needs of both episodes. That place was actually two locations: a coal delivery area at Philip Morris that, at one time, served the facility's steam generation plant (the site of Nazir's lair and tunnels for some of the chase), and the former Clariant Corporation dye factory, first used in the pilot.

"You're never going to find the look and vibe you want, as written in the script, in one place," Podeswa explains. It became a matter of mapping out which pieces of each scene would occur in which part of what facility. Podeswa created the right plan by drafting a rudimentary storyboard and scouting and discussing solutions with Klick and Kretschmer. "We scouted for a few days, going, 'Okay, will this work for that? And will that work for this? And how do we make it look like this belongs to this other part?' It's an invented geography."

An important scene in Ferland's episode is the one in which Nazir delivers his philosophy to Carrie. "We make a concerted effort to give our bad guys a point of view," Gansa explains, one with which Carrie obviously doesn't agree in the slightest. "This was two people in two very different worlds, having a conversation with each other, and who are ultimately at complete cross purposes."

TOP: "Broken Hearts" director Guy Ferland discusses a shot with cinematographer Nelson Cragg.

CENTER: Camera operators Nick Davidoff (left) and Bob Newcomb (right) capture the action as Carrie dashes down railroad tracks outside Clariant.

BOTTOM: "In Memorium" director Jeremy Podeswa (left) and cinematographer Nelson Cragg (center) discuss a setup, as camera operator Bob Newcomb listens.

The writers struggled with Nazir's speech to Carrie. Says Ferland, "Navid in particular was concerned that Nazir not come across as a one-dimensional bad guy. If Nazir's going to die for a cause, he wants someone to know the cause," even if it falls on deaf ears, adds Negahban. "It's his responsibility to explain himself. It's not his responsibility for someone to hear it."

One important consideration both directors had was the condition of their star: Claire Danes was, at this point, very pregnant. "I was really concerned, because there was a lot of running through tunnels and hand-to-hand combat with Nazir," Podeswa recalls. "There were things I thought would be beyond her ability in that condition, but she was incredible." Danes performed all but the most violent of stunts herself, even some of the hand-to-hand combat. "She's actually very good at it," the director says. "But between her stunt double and picture double, there were four people there in Claire's costume!"

Visual removal of Danes's "baby bump" was achieved with careful camera angles and visual effects, skills Podeswa had developed on an episode of *Boardwalk Empire.* For wide shots where her condition would be unavoidably visible, Danes was photographed first, typically followed by her non-pregnant photo double, Meredith Tingen, performing the same moves on set; and then a pass was made without Danes, to provide background image data for visual effects artists to use, where needed, of the same shot. Mike Leone's team at Lion VFX then combined the appropriate pieces—Danes's upper half, the double's midriff, and any missing background, to create a seamless, non-pregnant Carrie. Pregnancy for Carrie would have to wait another season.

Nazir eventually releases Carrie, after forcing Brody to assist in the killing of Walden. "Brody still has his priorities, and his main concern is Carrie," says Ferland. The scene is meant to finally give the audience a sense of victory for Brody. "So much of this show is about him being thwarted. It was good to give him a victory after all the craziness in his life. And Damian played it with just a little bit of relish, which was great."

The narcissistic Vice President can barely grasp what Brody is doing to him, so Brody spells it out: "Don't you get it? I'm killing you." "Walden's been blinded for so long by his romantic fantasy about this soldier. The betrayal is just outrageous," says Jamey Sheridan. "For Walden, it's like being killed by a son of his making. His own Frankenstein son."

A number of takes were filmed of varying lengths, including one in which Brody mentions Issa. But that one doesn't appear in the final edit. "The name Issa would have meant nothing to Walden," Gansa says. "It just felt like it was too much information to give Walden."

After her release, Carrie interrogates Roya, utilizing the "Saul Method" skills that had worked so successfully with Brody. But this interrogation ends with Roya ripping Carrie to shreds. "It's a seesaw of power," says Podeswa. "Roya's the one who's tied up, but then she turns the tables, and Carrie's vulnerability is exposed."

"It was a challenge, because it was my first time working with Claire, plus I was very sick with a high fever that day," actor Zuleikha Robinson remembers. She nonetheless portrays the seething hate that eventually erupts from Roya. "There was some Arabic that Zuleikha had to speak, which was difficult," Johannessen relates. "But she started repeating one phrase,

OPPOSITE: Death of a tyrant: Navid Negahban is prepared to be displayed as the deceased Abu Nazir.

ABOVE: Before and after visual effects test, illustrating removal of Claire Danes's "baby bump," as performed by Lion VFX.

BELOW: Standing in for the pregnant Claire Danes, when needed, during the filming of the action-packed "Broken Hearts" and "In Memorium" in Season 2, are (left to right): body double Caitlin Wolfe, stand-in Paula McLaughlin and stunt actor Abigail Martin.

> *"It is the end of an era for Carrie. It's a strange moment for Brody, too. You can love something and hate something at the same time."*
> — JEREMY PODEWSA

and it was so great, because you could just see that Roya was just this violent animal."

Carrie takes note of something Roya says and realizes that Nazir has never left the mill. So she returns to her team there, and, after an exciting pursuit, Nazir is killed. When his body is brought outside, Carrie asks to see it one last time. It is the end of an era for Carrie. "It's a very complicated moment," says Podeswa, "because she has been chasing him forever. And it's a bit of a 'Now what?' moment. 'He's gone, so where is my purpose? Where is my focus?' It's the closing of a chapter, but also with a weird loss in there, too."

It's a strange moment also for Brody, who receives the news while visiting his family in the safe house apartment. "Brody's relationship with Nazir has changed so much over the course of episodes," the director continues. "He has two contradictory emotions at once. You can love something and hate something at the same time."

Ultimately, says Gansa, "We wanted to play the moment as anticlimactic. We wanted to settle the audience with that anticlimax, because we knew what was coming next."

A NEW GROUND ZERO

FINALLY, BRODY IS FREE FROM NAZIR, free from his marriage, and he and Carrie can finally be together. Sounds perfect, right? Season 2 could have easily ended there. But this is *Homeland*.

The writers knew an explosion was coming. "Nazir was on a suicide mission," says showrunner Alex Gansa. "A lot of people asked, 'How was he going to get out of the country?' The whole point was that Nazir was never going to leave America." All of the pieces fit together perfectly into a masterful plan: Walden dies, Nazir is killed, and a memorial service would be packed with VIPs, ready to be slaughtered. "His plan all along was that, after his death, everybody would lower their guard." Now, Brody, instrumental in capturing the world's foremost terrorist, could be waved through security, along with a bomb.

But was Brody involved? "We wanted some people to think, 'My God, he must have been complicit,'" Gansa states. "It turns out he

TOP: Stunt performers Abigail Martin and Max Caulder experience the blast for Claire Danes and Damian Lewis in Saul's office. Note the cables attached to the actors, as they are "ratcheted" sharply backwards to portray the effect of the blast.

wasn't, and we didn't think he was. But we wanted to leave that not definitely answered."

Just as David Estes is delivering his speech, a massive explosion blasts through the glass auditorium wall, killing nearly everyone inside, including Estes, but sparing Carrie and Brody, who, bored with the proceedings, had slipped out just prior, to chat in Saul's office.

The explosion was filmed in a former cafeteria dining room at Cambridge, with 100 extras in various official/formal attire. Director Michael Cuesta filmed David Harewood addressing the assembly, while producer Michael Klick later filmed, with a second unit, Harewood's "explosive" reaction to the blast, as well as groupings of the guests in the auditorium, "tiled" through visual effects to appear as a much bigger crowd.

Up in Saul's office, Brody and Carrie also bear the brunt of the explosion—or, rather, Lewis's and Danes's stunt doubles, Max Calder and Abigail Martin, do. (Despite the doubles, Lewis nonetheless injured his back lifting Danes, briefly halting filming of the scene.) After coming to, Carrie goes through a huge emotional swing, from damning Brody for causing the explosion, to realizing and accepting his innocence. "That was one of the hardest scenes I ever directed on *Homeland*," says Cuesta. "We did a lot of takes, because Claire really wanted to find the emotional truth of that scene. She had to turn on a dime there, emotionally. It wasn't easy."

At the time of the explosion, Saul is overseeing the burial at sea of Abu Nazir, a proper Muslim rite, modeled on the one given to Osama bin Laden. The sequence was shot a few days after principal photography for the season had been completed. Mandy Patinkin joined the "dead" Navid Negahban, an imam (Haythem Noor), and two Muslim sailors aboard the USS *Yorktown*, berthed on display as a museum in Charleston, South Carolina. "We shot it on Election Day, November 6, and we finished it in time for me to fly back to New York and vote," Cuesta recalls.

Prop master Gillian Albinski had three identical 200-pound dummies built to represent the wrapped body of Nazir, weighted with concrete so they would drop over the side feet first, and tied together with a rebar armature to make sure they wouldn't break apart on impact with the water. "After we had dropped them in, over several takes, the tide changed and the current was too strong, so we couldn't retrieve them," says producer Michael Klick. "I can just see them dredging one day there and coming up with these three shrouded bodies!"

The murky waters prevented Klick, shooting in an underwater unit, from capturing the bodies as they entered the water, so Albinski had three eighteen-inch dummies made, and they were photographed the following day at a swimming pool back in Charlotte—the pool in Coulwood where production designer John Kretschmer swam as a boy.

Following the explosion, Saul Berenson is left as the surviving officer in charge of the CIA. Viewers see him stunned as he observes the devastation. The rubble pile was built by Kretschmer on a parking lot at Philip Morris. The enormous temporary "morgue" was created in one of the six former cigarette assembly rooms at the plant. "It felt kind of fitting," Gansa remarks. "A lot of death was perpetrated from those rooms. It was an interesting confluence of location and storytelling."

The breathtaking imagery of the bodies laid out was inspired by a photo Cuesta had seen of corpses similarly laid out following a tsunami in Southeast Asia. "It was haunting, because they usually lay them out in dark body bags, but these body bags were white. They looked almost like ghosts."

The production originally called for fifty extras to portray the wrapped corpses (again "tiled," photographed in different positions in the room and assembled later in visual effects to create the appearance of a large grouping). But Albinski suggested a much more efficient method. "Extras are expensive, but blow-up dolls are cheap," she says. However, they were hard to find on November 2—three days after Halloween—so full mannequins were also used,

TOP: Mandy Patinkin and Michael Cuesta discuss the scene, aboard the historic USS *Yorktown*, berthed in Charleston, South Carolina.

CENTER: Saul officiates at the burial at sea of Abu Nazir.

BOTTOM: Prop master Gillian Albinski readies an 18-inch miniature of Nazir's corpse for "burial" at the Coulwood Pool in Charlotte.

TOP: Stirring imagery of hundeds of CIA dead—actually blow-up dolls and manequins—inside one of the former Philip Morris cigarette assembly rooms.

BOTTOM: Model detailing the set design of the aftermath of the Langley explosion.

augmented with 200 additional mannequin body parts, which the team spent three days painting black and bloodied prior to the shoot.

The completed setup was startling. "I remember walking into that room and seeing all those bodies laid out, and just having the breath knocked out of me," says Gansa. "It was such an iconic image."

Saul's recitation of the Jewish Kaddish prayer of mourning was an idea Patinkin suggested, to which Cuesta quickly agreed. "He's mourning, but he also has to do his job," Cuesta notes. Carrie returns to the scene in that moment, and Saul, having thought her to be among the dead, hears her voice and hardly believes his ears. "She's like a ghost," the director says. The scene was the last one Danes filmed for the season.

Brody is quickly determined to be the most likely culprit of the bombing. "It was interesting to us to flip the situation from what it was at the end of Season 1," says Chip Johannessen.

"At the end of Season 2, he's being blamed for something he didn't do, and when he started the season, he wasn't being blamed for something he was about to do. It felt like nice bookends to his journey."

Before returning to the CIA blast site, Carrie helps Brody escape by taking him to the Canadian border. The border scene was filmed on Neck Road in beautiful, historic Rural Hill in Huntersville, North Carolina. Interestingly, in the first draft of the script, Carrie crossed the border with Brody, and the two went on the run together. But, Gansa says, "We read the draft, and thought there was no way on earth she would be going with Brody, when the guy who's responsible for killing all those people is still out there. She's a career intelligence officer. Being with Brody paled in comparison to her duty as a CIA officer. So we sent her back to be with Saul, to live in the ruin and the failure of their operation together."

CIA Ground Zero, as built on the parking lot at Philip Morris.

SEASON THREE

★ FIFTY-EIGHT DAYS AFTER

the Langley bombing that ended Season 2, Carrie Mathison finds herself testifying before a Senate subcommittee about the disaster, headed by the unsympathetic Senator Andrew Lockhart. He presses Carrie about her involvement, and, more important, that of Brody, who was last seen, at the end of Season 2, being dropped off by Carrie at the Canadian border. When someone slips Lockhart a copy of Brody's secret plea deal, he's able to catch his witness off guard.

Saul, now the CIA's acting director, watches Carrie's testimony on television in his new office, which has a clear view of the still-horrifying "pit" outside his window at Langley. Dar Adal, who watches with Saul, suggests that Carrie's instability could become an asset to protect the agency, which is now under fire from Lockhart. Saul resists. But later, as a horrified Carrie watches, Saul testifies before Lockhart's subcommittee and places much of the blame for the bombing on her instability and involvement with Brody. Furious, Carrie approaches a reporter to tell her side of the story, but before she can finish, she's suddenly apprehended and taken to a mental institution.

In his first major move since taking control of the agency, Saul supervises a mission that simultaneously kills six terrorists involved with the bombing. With the CIA's ranks decimated by the bombing, Saul brings in a young, new financial analyst, Fara Sherazi, an Iranian-American, who identifies the mastermind of the bombing: Majid Javadi, Deputy Chief, Intelligence Directorate for the Iranian Revolutionary Guard Corps. She also uncovers the fact that Javadi has been skimming millions of dollars from his government. Saul, who knows Javadi from his days in Tehran, intends to use this information against his former associate to force his cooperation.

Dana Brody returns home from a treatment center, where she has been recovering from a suicide attempt. While there, she has connected romantically with a young man named Leo, who is recovering from having witnessed his brother's apparent suicide. Unable to stomach returning to her old life in the Brody home, Dana steals her mom's car and helps Leo break out of the institution, and the two go on the run to start a new life together. But Dana soon learns Leo's secret, that he actually had a role in killing his brother, and will not tolerate another liar in her life. When the two are caught, she returns home alone, later changes her last name, and goes to live on her own.

Brody, meanwhile, shows up in Venezuela with gunshot wounds to the stomach, courtesy of Columbian soldiers, and is brought to the Tower of David, a vertical slum within an unfinished high-rise in Caracas. This "community" is run by a local warlord—and friend of Carrie's—named El Niño. One of the Tower's many exiles is a discredited doctor, a pedophile named Graham. He treats Brody with the only available painkiller, heroin, to which Brody soon becomes addicted.

Carrie has been unable to find a way out of the mental hospital; but she is soon visited by Paul Franklin, an associate of a lawyer, Leland Bennett, who gets her released in exchange for help for his client. The client, in this case, is the Islamic Republic of Iran, represented by Javadi who suggests she turn against her country and offer him CIA secrets. However, as it is further revealed, Javadi has been duped by Saul and Carrie. They have concocted the complicated ruse of her insanity—and betrayal by Saul—to entrap him. Carrie threatens to expose Javadi's government embezzlement to the Iranians if he doesn't cooperate with her and Saul. Javadi agrees to return to Iran on behalf of the CIA, but not before taking his own revenge for past betrayals by brutally slaughtering his ex-wife with a broken wine bottle. Passed up for the permanent directorship of the Agency in favor of Lockhart, Saul pursues a plan. Now that he's forced Javadi back to Iran, he'll use Brody to assassinate Javadi's boss, Danesh Akbari, to allow Javadi to rise to the top of the government and finally effect positive policy change in the country.

Saul retrieves the addicted Brody from Caracas and quickly rehabilitates him before Lockhart can take office and shut down the operation. With the help of a Special Ops team, Brody returns to Iran, under the pretense of requesting political asylum, and kills Akbari as planned. Carrie attempts to help Brody escape, but Lockhart and Adal enable Javadi to capture Brody. This advances Saul and Carrie's larger plan intact, but Brody is hanged in a public square for killing Akbari, and a distraught Carrie, who it has been revealed, is pregnant with Brody's child, returns home.

Carrie makes peace with Lockhart and accepts an assignment from him to head a new post in the Middle East. Saul, meanwhile, has decided to work as a private contractor and to begin a new life with his wife, Mira. Before they move into their new roles, Carrie and Saul attend a ceremony together that honors fallen CIA agents with stars engraved in the building's lobby. Unable to convince Lockhart to place a star in Brody's honor, Carrie draws one in herself with a pen, as her own memorial.

A RUSE IS COOKED

IN MID-DECEMBER 2012, THE *HOMELAND* writers got together for three days to begin answering some big questions. "We had excommunicated Brody to some far-flung land, and we had just blown up the CIA," says showrunner Alex Gansa. "So we had a lot to figure out."

Clearly, a reaction to the CIA bombing was in order, but what would it be? The team would often begin their story planning by talking about recent books or articles that had caught their interest. Writer Chip Johannessen had recently been reading about the return and assassination of former Pakistani Prime Minister Benazir Bhutto, killed in 2007, and this prompted a discussion about a returning political leader. "The idea we developed centered around an agent like Carrie trying to protect a leader who had been in exile and who was returning to his country for the noblest of reasons," Gansa explains, "coming back to reinstate some sort of democratic, Western values to a country that needed it." An assassination would take

place, and the focus would then move to who was responsible, and what was the CIA's role.

This would make a good story for Carrie, but the writers struggled to find a way to work Brody into the narrative, so the idea was abandoned in favor of one involving a regime change. "The idea was to allow Saul to make a policy change on behalf of the United States, against the country that perpetrated the attack on the CIA," Johannessen states.

When the team reassembled at writer Henry Bromell's house in Santa Monica at the end of January, Bromell and Johannessen began mapping out the season. "We had a bunch of stuff, but it was incoherent." Then Gansa suggested the idea of a ruse.

"The ruse idea was mostly generated out of a conversation that I had with our intelligence consultants in D.C. before the season started," Gansa recalls. An attack like the one at Langley would have required the country that perpetrated it to use a proxy, like Abu Nazir, so that the United States couldn't identify a specific country to retaliate against. But someone in the government would have had to order the attack and hire Nazir. "Our task," says Gansa, "then became to create a character inside Iran who was difficult to flush out, who hadn't been seen in years." That character became Majid Javadi. "So then it was a matter of figuring out, 'How would Saul and Carrie flush him out?'"

The answer was to dangle a piece of bait that Javadi couldn't resist. "That bait was Carrie herself, an intelligence officer who was profoundly close to Saul, whom Javadi knew well, and who might give Javadi precious information about American intelligence work around the globe." Gansa was a big fan of John le Carré's classic spy novel *The Spy Who Came in from the Cold* and liked the idea of sending Carrie in to do the job. "With the CIA coming under attack by Lockhart and his Senate Select Committee, Carrie could be scapegoated by the CIA, defamed in front of the committee, try to fight back and ultimately be discredited and disgraced," says Gansa, making her appear to be a perfect target to be turned.

The hearing room used for Carrie's testimony before the committee was actually located in the stately North Carolina Supreme Court building in Raleigh, a two-hour drive from Charlotte.

"I felt it was very important not to set hearings like this in little conference rooms, as they were scripted," says director Lesli Linka Glatter. Glatter took over as *Homeland*'s producing director after Season 2 when Michael Cuesta had moved on to direct, *Kill the Messenger*, a feature film starring Jeremy Renner. "I felt like you needed to visually feel the weight of the government coming down on Carrie." As actor Tracy Letts (Sen. Lockhart) says, "It's great to sit up there on that bench, with all these guys around you, and look down on your prey."

Production designer John Kretschmer traveled to Raleigh and was immediately taken with the beauty of the circa 1940 structure. It took some doing to get the clerk of the court to agree to allow the production to shoot in the space. "I eventually had to drive up there and sit in a circle with six justices and answer questions,"

OPPOSITE: The North Carolina Supreme Court, as seen by production designer John Kretschmer during the team's scouting visit on April 24, six weeks before the June 3 filming date.

THIS PAGE, BOTTOM: Director Lesli Linka Glatter and cinematographer David Klein on a scouting trip to see the North Carolina Supreme Court building, which appears as a Senate hearing room in "Tin Man Is Down."

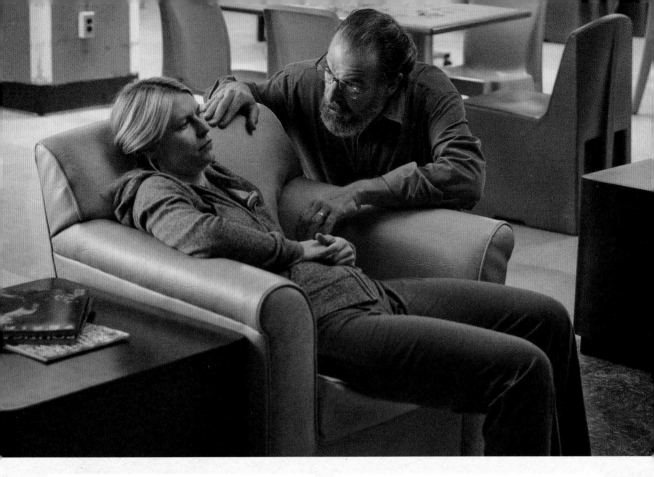

recalls executive producer Michael Klick. "They were very protective of the space."

The court historian was even more protective of an odd piece of furniture, a long, old wood bench used by attorneys to lay out evidence and briefs, which was falling apart and needed to be moved out of the way. Says Kretschmer, "I had my finish carpenters come in and repair it, make it good as new, and then we jacked it up and rolled it to the back." State legislators were invited to watch the filming, and, after the dust settled, Klick received a nice letter from the clerk acknowledging how well it all had gone.

Saul's testimony at the public hearing where he publicly discredits Carrie was filmed in a different location, Heaton Hall in the Cornwell Center complex of the Myers Park Baptist Church in Charlotte. "It's a big complex, the kind of place you see in a prosperous Baptist church in the South," Kretschmer explains. "We had to fit 200 people in there. And we built the bench at which the committee is seated."

When Saul testifies, Carrie realizes for the first time what she's gotten herself into. "It's one thing to say, 'I'll take the blame for all this as a way of drawing this man out of Iran,'" says Gansa. "It's another thing to see it happening on television, and to watch Saul publicly destroy her character."

In order to fool Javadi, and the rest of the world, both Saul and Carrie have to behave in ways that appear real, no matter what it takes. "The intelligence officers we consult with explained to me that the best operations are always ninety-five percent true," Gansa explains. "Saul and Carrie have to behave as if this is actually happening, to make it completely and utterly credible that she is being destroyed and 'controversialized' by the CIA."

Saul's placing Carrie in a mental institution hasn't been planned by the two conspirators, but it's a believable response by Saul to Carrie approaching the media. "Saul has to behave as if Carrie is a loose cannon rolling around on deck," says Gansa. "It has to be credible to the people around him, like Dar Adal, that this woman is dangerous."

Scenes of Carrie at the Manassas County Hospital were filmed at the Liberty Nursing & Rehabilitation Center in Charlotte. The location had been used in Season 1 for scenes of Carrie in the hospital. "It's very difficult to find hospitals to shoot in, particularly active ones," says Kretschmer. Adds producer Michael Klick, "Everybody's thinking of the hospital in *One Flew Over the Cuckoo's Nest*, with its tall ceilings and tall windows. But there aren't a lot of old empty places sitting around." Despite the challenges, Kretschmer managed to create the perfect look for the hospital. "It's County: no money, grungy, dirty, real life," he says. Adds Glatter, "It was so depressing, that old nursing home. And at a county mental institution, there are just a lot of people being warehoused." When Saul finally comes to visit her, Carrie has only three words for him: "Fuck you, Saul." "I think this has turned out to be a lot harder than what she had ever imagined," Glatter notes. "For her it's, 'Yes, I agreed to do this, but I'm in here, and you're out there.'"

When Carrie is finally released from the hospital, thanks to lawyer Leland Bennett, she makes her way to Saul's house, where it is finally revealed to the audience that the whole matter was indeed a ruse—and a successful one. This reveal, however, doesn't happen until Episode 4. "Again, it had to be believable," says Gansa. "It had to be a significant amount of time so you'd buy the idea that the deputy chief of Iran's intelligence service would be fooled, but also enough time to fool the audience. Otherwise the idea wouldn't work. You had to feel and see the depth of the consequences, that Carrie would be desperate enough to bargain with the devil."

The reveal was as big an emotional release for the actors, as it is for the audience. "That was probably one of the most difficult days of shooting that Claire has experienced," Gansa adds. "Both Mandy and Claire found it very difficult to contain their emotions. You felt the pain Carrie had suffered, and knew it was real."

BOTTOM: Director Lesli Linka Glatter discusses Saul's testimony with Mandy Patinkin.

A LOSS IN THE FAMILY

On March 18, 2013, the *Homeland* family received a shock when the most beloved member of their writing team, Henry Bromell, died of a sudden heart attack at age sixty-five.

"We had just written the first episode and thought we were off to such a strong start, and then this enormous personal tragedy occurred," says show-runner Alex Gansa. "Losing Henry stopped us in our tracks."

Television writing staffs are sometimes contentious, at best, but the *Homeland* staff is truly a family. "All of us had become so close, and had bonded over the tremendous success of the show," Gansa says. "We have genuine affection and respect for each other."

"We would have breakfast on the Westside and hang out, just chat about stuff," recalls writer Alex Cary. "When I first met him, Henry had a new family with his wife, and he was addicted to his family. And he had this amazing office behind his house, lined with books. I mean, amazing books. He was an artist who was made for this kind of work. He was fascinated and excited in his approach to characters. He was both a storytelling professor and a man with a little boy sense about spy stories, all at once."

The sadness felt after Bromell's death was formidable. "I don't think anybody went back to work for a month," says Gansa. "There was a memorial service and mourning to be done. But, unfortunately, there was also a television show to be written and produced."

When the team reconvened, they didn't meet in the modern building on the Fox lot where they had written the first two seasons. "The ghost of Henry was too present there," says Gansa. They moved into the Old Writers' Building on the Fox lot. "We couldn't sit in the story room anymore, it was just too painful. And there's no question that the sorrow of that event infused the writing staff and the mood of the stories in Season 3." Bromell's legacy on the show was far from forgotten. In September, he received a posthumous Emmy for Season 2's "Q&A," an episode that is often regarded as one of *Homeland*'s best.

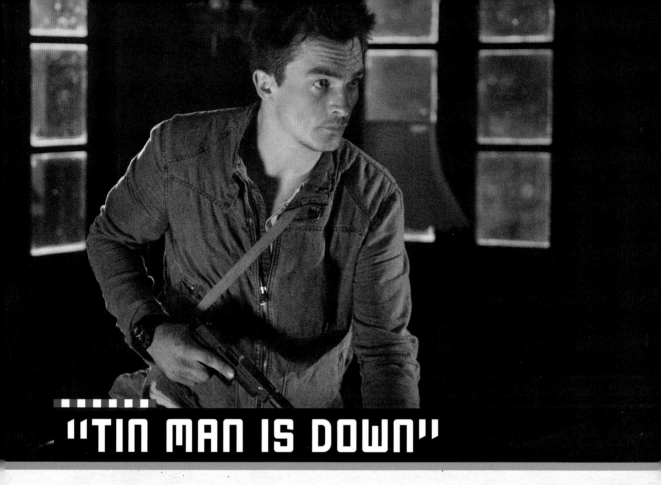

"TIN MAN IS DOWN"

IN MID-JUNE, A MONTH INTO FILMING Season 3, the production shifted briefly to Puerto Rico, to film two stories set in Caracas, Venezuela: the Episode 1 "Tin Man Is Down" action sequence in which Quinn kills the banker, Cedeño, and the Episode 3 "Tower of David" scenes of Brody's hell-away-from-home.

"Our first choice, of course, would have been Caracas," says producer Michael Klick, "but that wasn't gonna happen, both from a practical standpoint, and for safety. The studio didn't want to take the risk, which was probably a good idea." Other options included Mexico and Brazil.

Production designer John Kretschmer took a scouting trip to Puerto Rico in late May with Klick and Fox 21 production executive Nissa Diederich, who found locations plentiful. "The San Juan cityscape played really well for Caracas," Kretschmer notes. "We found everything we needed," particularly in Old San Juan.

The crew also filmed in the seaside town of Arecibo. Its La Iglesia de San Felipe, a Catholic church, was used for the mosque in which Brody attempts to find refuge in Episode 3, "Tower of David."

Director Clark Johnson shot "Tower of David" first (see pages 134–137), after which director Lesli Linka Glatter arrived with Season 3's new director of photography, David Klein, to film the action sequences with Rupert Friend for "Tin Man Is Down." While Glatter was filming the dramatic scenes, Klick simultaneously ran a second unit to shoot Rupert Friend playing Quinn driving through Old San Juan on a motorcycle. In this scene, Quinn is following Cedeño's car, on which he's attempting to attach a magnetic bomb that he has built to blow it up.

By the way, for the most part, Friend is driving the bike. "I've been riding since I was about sixteen or seventeen," Friend reveals. "The stuntman had a holiday." Notes Klick, "It wasn't high speed or anything. He just had to follow the car on those wonderful narrow streets of the old city. But Rupert owns a motorcycle and rides it to work every day in Charlotte."

The footage was shot at night simultaneously with Glatter's own shoot at another location, Friend splitting his time between stunt driving and acting that evening. "In the previous season, we strongly intimated that Quinn was somebody who worked the darker side of the intelligence business," says showrunner Alex Gansa. "That he was somebody who got his hands dirty, and we don't even know his real name. But you never actually saw him do anything. So we thought it was time."

Quinn is about to bomb Cedeño's car, when he realizes Cedeño's young son is in the back seat. So, he changes plans, opting instead to quietly enter Cedeño's house (San Juan's beautiful Casa de España) and shoot the banker. "He's a killer with a conscience," says Gansa. "He views his profession through a moral lens." But fate is against him. When Quinn is surprised by a sound in the house, he shoots and mistakenly kills the boy after all.

"That idea was suggested by James Yoshimura," says writer Chip Johannessen. "We were wondering what could happen there, and he said, 'Kill the kid.' We thought it would be interesting if Quinn went into the house because he was trying not to kill the kid, and then it happened anyway."

This accident affects Quinn profoundly. "He goes to Philadelphia and finds Julia and his son," Friend informs. "He breaks down and tells her he can't handle what he's done." As things continue, and Quinn observes the goings-on with Carrie, he begins to question his vocation even more. "He witnesses the ruthlessness and appetite the CIA have for eating their own," Gansa says. "He begins to realize that the things he's asked to do don't lead to any loyalty."

As Glatter explains, "Quinn is someone who's stuffed down his emotions for years, and all of a sudden, he's not able to do that in quite the same way. He's seriously questioning what is going on in the CIA now. Between watching what's going on with Carrie and the CIA bombing, and now killing the kid, this guy, who's basically an assassin, is suddenly thinking, 'I don't know if I can do this anymore.'" Adds Friend, "In this season, we begin to explore the beginning of his work no longer just being a blind order. If I am a guy who kills bad guys, and I gave up my wife and my kid, I need to be absolutely certain who the bad guys are and who the good guys are, and make sure I'm not working for the wrong side."

BOTTOM: An avid motorcyclist, Rupert Friend arrives for work on location on his own motorcycle during filming of Season 2's "I'll Fly Away."

SENATOR LOCKHART

AFTER THE BOMBING OF LANGLEY, SAUL Berenson needs friends. Unfortunately, Senator Andrew Lockhart is not one.

"We needed to find an adversary for Carrie and Saul, somebody who is driving at the truth and suspects something is amiss," says Alex Gansa. That would be Lockhart.

"A couple of hundred people have been killed at the CIA," says Tracy Letts, who plays the senator. "So when living members of the CIA say, 'Nah, we got this,' you want to look at them and say, 'Actually, it's real clear that you don't have it.' It's up to somebody else to get to the bottom of this."

Tracy Letts, a Tony–winning Broadway actor and Pulitzer Prize–winning playwright (for *August: Osage County*), was spotted by Gansa in a performance of *Who's Afraid of Virginia Woolf?* and seemed perfect for the role. "We needed an actor who could deliver a mouthful of exposition believably, and we got way more than that," Gansa explains.

Letts is perfectly comfortable spouting Lockhart's beliefs about the CIA. "That's because I agree with him. He's the one guy asking for a little accountability from this organization. I pursued his line of inquiry with Saul and Carrie with fervor, because I felt Lockhart had a good point. His questions deserved answering."

Lockhart seems closed to anything Saul has to offer, prompting Saul to keep him out of the loop, and thus out of the way. "When Saul tells him about the regime change plan with Javadi, and that Javadi's been on U.S. soil and Saul hasn't told anyone, that just confirms what Lockhart suspected," says Letts, who feels Lockhart's attitude isn't without reason. "The deaths of all those people at the CIA helped close his mind about Saul and his ideas about what's best."

Because he has no intelligence background, Lockhart is at odds with Saul regarding his approach of using agents on the ground versus electronic surveillance. "That mirrors a real debate inside the agency," Gansa notes. "How risky is human intelligence versus electronic intelligence gathering? What is more valuable? Those are the questions Lockhart represents."

DANA AND LEO

DANA BRODY HAS BEEN THROUGH A LOT. If not for her father, she would have simply gone through all of the teenage anxieties kids normally go through. But she's had plenty more, eventually pushing her to the breaking point.

"It was important to us to shine a harsh light on the collateral damage of Brody's purported actions," explains showrunner Alex Gansa. "And ultimately, that led us to a place where Dana felt betrayed and lied to at the deepest level," attempting to kill herself not long after the Langley bombing. "Dana stood up for him and believed in him," says actor Morgan Saylor. "She gave him her heart and believed in who he was and what he stood for, even to the point of accepting his religion. Having that rug pulled out from under her was huge. So when I read the first script for Season 3, and found out what she'd tried to do, it felt very real. It wouldn't have felt fair to her, as a character, if we'd just picked up with Dana back in everyday life."

When we meet her again in Episode 1, Dana has just finished a round of inpatient treatment at Idylwood Rehabilitation Center (most scenes of which were filmed at Myers Park Baptist Church's Cornwell Center, the same location where Saul's public hearing was shot in the same episode). Her treatment has been a success, Saylor says. "I have a scene with Morena, where Dana finally tells her mom that 'Dad ruined our lives.' I think, in her therapy, she finally figured out that it was his fault."

Dana not only changes her last name, but decides to move out, the latter something which actually paralleled Saylor's own life. "I turned 18 while we were filming Season 3, and I moved out of my parents' house in Atlanta and moved to New York," she relates. "We both grew up at the same time."

While at Idylwood, Dana has fallen in love with a charismatic young man named Leo Carras, played by twenty-six-year-old British-born actor Sam Underwood, in Idylwood apparently for having witnessed his brother's suicide. Dana returns and helps Leo break out, and the two go on a road trip to begin life anew.

"Leo doesn't judge Dana based on her 'infamy' in the media," Underwood says. "He sees beyond that. Leo really is in love with her and wants to protect her. He convinces Dana that they can start fresh, that the outside world really doesn't matter."

In keeping with Dana's evolving maturity, there are even love scenes between her and Leo, a change that mirrored the growth of the actress portraying her. "When she shot her first episode, Morgan was just 15," Alex Gansa recalls. "She was a kid, and now she's on the verge of being an adult. And Dana is in the middle of her sexual awakening."

Saylor and director Lesli Linka Glatter had many discussions about what she was comfortable doing onscreen for such scenes. "Of course, one wants to handle something like that really carefully," says Glatter. "We talked about how we were going to do it, and I choreographed it with her and Sam, so they would both feel as comfortable as possible. It's very romantic and sensual, without exposing anything."

Dana and Leo enjoy an "on-the-run" road trip, until Dana discovers there's more to Leo's story than he's told her: that he was actually involved in his brother's death. He's yet another liar in her life, which is something she can't accept.

"He had been looking for the right time to tell her but never had the guts," Underwood explains. "That scene was tough to film. It was an emotional roller coaster, going from denial to anger to shame."

"That was the idea behind that character," says writer Chip Johannessen. "We wanted to put somebody in Dana's life that was the one good thing in her life, because her father betrayed her, and then have him do the same thing."

The writers considered having the two commit a double suicide while on the road, Gansa says. "But that wouldn't have left anything to motivate Brody to come back to life himself. Dana plays a crucial role in motivating him to complete his mission."

SAUL AND MIRA

OVER THE COURSE OF THREE SEASONS, fans have seen Saul Berenson and his wife, Mira (Sarita Choudhury), close, distant, truly apart, and, finally, truly together.

The problem was simple, says showrunner Alex Gansa: "Saul's wife is the CIA." Because of his workload and commitment, "the relationship had stagnated and had ceased being a physical relationship. They had become 'friends at home.'" It wasn't enough for Mira, and she had her own professional aspirations to pursue.

In all of the darkness of Saul's world, Mira has been the one soft place to which he could always return. "She provided him a lot of comfort, but she wasn't getting what she needed," Gansa notes. This prompted her move to India in Season 1. "When she wound up leaving, it created a big, big hole in Saul's life, one that he was unable to replace. I think it isolated him more and more as a person." Mira was born in India, is clearly well-educated, someone who, like Dar Adal in his professional life, can go toe-to-toe with Saul.

"She's a truth teller to him. And oftentimes, he's not particularly pleased to hear it," Gansa says. The couple, over the years, had moved around the world, from post to post, eventually settling in Washington, D.C., a few years before we meet them, though Mira found it hard to establish friendships in the city.

While living overseas during their split, she has connected with Alain Bernard, whom we meet in Season 3, played by William Abadie, but he has bonded with her solely for intelligence purposes. "Their relationship was, by no means, a betrayal of Saul, at least in our minds, seeing as Mira and Saul were separated," says Gansa. "But Alain's motives were not honorable, to say the least."

Saul, during Season 3, struggles to muster the desire to fight for his wife, even when she made it clear she wants him to. "It's not until he begins to have the successes he does at the agency that he really gets his mojo back," Gansa points out. "It's not until then, when he has claimed his job, that he also returns and claims Mira."

FARA SHERAZI

ANOTHER NEW CHARACTER IN SEASON 3 is Fara Sherazi, a financial analyst for the CIA, played by the beautiful Nazanin Boniadi, an actor who had been considered the previous season for the part of Roya Hammad.

Says showrunner Alex Gansa, "In order to counter the preponderance of Muslim terrorists on the show we wanted to create a Muslim character with an entirely different, heroic perspective." Fara offers her services to the CIA even in the face of danger to her family back home. Her courage is depicted in the scenes of Fara talking to her elderly father, from whom she keeps her current vocation a secret.

While serving her new country, Fara remains true to her religion and its customs, even to the point of wearing a hijab, the headscarf that Muslim women wear. "I think it takes a degree of brazenness for her to wear her headscarf into that building, and to wear it proudly," Gansa says. "She's saying, 'Yes, I'm a Muslim, but I'm

not party to what is going on. I had nothing to do with that. I'm here to help.'"

The writers turn American prejudice toward Muslims on its head in the scene when the character is introduced in Episode 2. Writer Chip Johannessen explains, "When she's entering the building, the way we shot it, she appears to have a mysterious briefcase and she has this headscarf. People look at her, and it creates this expectation that maybe she's bad. But, of course, she's anything but."

When it seems to Saul that Fara isn't pushing herself enough in her work, he gives her an uncharacteristic chewing out. "He's just really frustrated and stressed from everything that's been going on," Johannessen notes. "But it seemed to me that was probably something he had done with Carrie when she was younger, too."

Fara briefly tears up, and then gets back to work. "His outburst to her is utterly inappropriate," says Gansa. "But she doesn't buckle under it. She stands proud, and then, through her work, makes Saul proud."

"TOWER OF DAVID"

SO WHAT TO DO WITH BRODY? He was last seen at the Canadian border, saying good-bye to Carrie. Should the writers find yet another way to connect the two in Season 3? "We knew we didn't want to repeat the relationship beats that we had already used," says writer Chip Johannessen. "And Brody was the most wanted man in the world, so that meant that he had to be in hiding." The writers also decided that Brody would not appear until a few episodes into the season. "The network wanted to see him earlier, but we wanted to make his reappearance feel significant, and pushing it back a few episodes was a cool way to do that."

The question was, where was he? "Carrie had devised an escape route for herself, in case things in America went south for her," showrunner Alex Gansa explains. "She herself was not aware where that 'underground railroad' would have taken her. She sent Brody off into the hands of these people whom she trusted, but she didn't know where he wound up." What she did know was that any attempt to reach out to him would tip off those looking for him and divulge his whereabouts.

The initial idea the team came up with was to put Brody in a lush Southeast Asian jungle, with bountiful supplies of sex and drugs, as one might find a character in a novel by spymaster Graham Greene. "That felt really dated to us and phony, plus there was nothing for him to do," Johannessen admits. "We needed to put more pressure on him."

The writers had all recently read a fascinating article in *The New Yorker* by Jon Lee Anderson about the so-called Tower of David, an unfinished forty-five-story skyscraper in Caracas, Venezuela, begun in 1990 by investor David Brillembourg, and whose construction was halted in 1994 due to a banking crisis. Squatters eventually moved in, and the building now houses more than 3000 people in what is essentially a vertical slum, run by armed hoodlums, led by Alexander "El Niño" Daza. "It's like a municipality," says actor Damian

Lewis. "They run their own school system and policing system—it's all corrupt, of course. But it functions, in an autocratic way."

Writer James Yoshimura suggested the Tower as the perfect place for Brody to end up, and the team agreed. Henry Bromell was due to write the episode, and had completed an outline, but when he passed away, the episode was left without a writer. "I missed him a lot," recalls Johannessen, "and I wanted, as a gift to him, to write the piece on his behalf and credit him. And he was incredibly proud of his son, Will, who's also a good writer. So I wrote the Caracas stuff, channeling Henry as best I could, and Will did the scenes about Carrie. It ended up the one chance for a father-and-son credit, which was something Henry had really wanted."

With filming in Caracas out of the question, the issue became where to find a building similar to the Tower of David. "We needed to find a half-finished skyscraper that would be safe enough to shoot in, where we could see a vista," notes director Lesli Linka Glatter. While searching online, Fox 21 production executive Nissa Diederich came upon a thirteen-story high-rise in Puerto Rico that, like the Tower of David, had been abandoned midway through construction. "It had sat fallow for three or four years, and it was just two blocks from our production office in San Juan," says executive producer Michael Klick. "It was perfect for us." Adds director Clark Johnson, "It was half finished, and we made it more half finished."

Production designer John Kretschmer took his lead from a book about the Tower of David, *Torre David.* "It's almost an encyclopedia about that world," he says. "It was a perfect blueprint to work from." Veteran construction coordinator Roger Scruggs was brought in to supervise construction of sets. "We even built the exterior construction elevator you see on the outside of the building," Klick says.

"The main thing I was looking to show was the domesticity there," relates Johnson. "Kretschmer, Klick, Alex, and Chip and I put all our energies into creating a progression, as you go up. There's this doctor doing weird shit in the basement, and then Brody goes upstairs, and it's bright, it's morning, and there are domestic sounds of people making breakfast, and this beautiful young girl is sitting looking at him." The world worked. "The sets were brilliant," says Lewis. "It really felt like a working slum, ten stories above the ground."

Like the real building, there were no outside walls or handrails, making filming dangerous,

Director Clark Johnson confers with Damian Lewis in the "Tower of David" location.

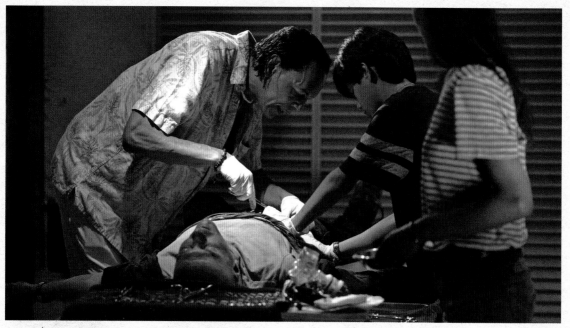

especially on windy days. "There was a terrific wind that howled down the corridors," Lewis recalls. "If you lost your footing and were near the edge, you could get blown out of the building. We had a lot of safety meetings about that, to make sure everybody was kept safe."

Tending to the gaping wounds in Brody's gut is a rather slimy character, the Tower's very own Dr. Graham (named, of course, for Graham Greene). Scripted to read almost as a washed-up Peter O'Toole type, Gansa says, "We thought we were going to cast some dissolute old English actor. In fact, we looked at a lot of them," and even considered a younger one—Claire Danes's husband, Hugh Dancy.

But Clark Johnson had worked for a number of years with a D.C.-based actor named Erik Dellums, who had portrayed Luther Mahoney on *Homicide: Life on the Street*, and suggested him for the role. "Clark really didn't tell me anything about the character," the actor recalls, least of all that he was a pedophile. "It certainly wasn't written for a six-foot-six-and-a-half-inch black guy," he laughs. Notes Johnson, "The audience needs to be wondering, 'What's this guy doing here?' With Erik Dellums, you wonder, and you get a creepier character. He's really interesting—in fact, we were all afraid he might just be a little too interesting!" Notes Gansa, "Clark and Chip were really pushing for him. And Erik came in and did the most bizarre audition I think I've ever seen. It was odd and singular, crazily effeminate and profoundly disturbing. He really came across as a denizen of hell."

Dellums saw Graham as a London-educated physician who had done his residency in the States, and who would have been successful if not for his predilection for young boys (such as nine-year-old Paco, who assists him around the Tower). "Graham himself had been molested at Paco's age. He would go from one prestigious gig to another, until he was found out, and he just started running," the actor relates. "Ultimately, he was gallivanting off to third-world countries," finally ending up at the Tower of David, a place where he can practice his warped behavior unchallenged. "He could be accepted in the Tower, because he's also a damned good doctor and the only one they could get," Johnson says.

"He's a very poetic character," Lewis observes. "He's a lost, tragic soul."

Graham, like El Niño, the de facto warlord of the Tower of David, has some firm words for Brody regarding the permanency of his stay there. The Tower is indeed Brody's last stop. "Anybody that comes into this place with an illusion that they're one day going to pack up and leave, that it's just a temporary experience, is someone that Graham dismisses with sarcasm," Dellums says. "Graham thought the same thing himself." As Johnson notes, "You're not going to get up one day and go get your old job back. That goes for both Brody and Carrie."

The heroin Graham gives Brody as a pain-killer doesn't help matters, Johnson adds. "Brody doesn't want to become a junkie. But it's a metaphor for the hopelessness of his situation." Adds Lewis, "I believe that Brody could take solace in something like that, and Brody succumbs to it."

Johnson filmed several days at the Tower for his episode. Then, on June 18, he was joined by Glatter, who had just arrived. After Johnson filmed a foggy Brody watching a thief take his belongings, Glatter shot a scene with another visitor, Mandy Patinkin, in which El Niño brings Saul into Brody's room to see Brody. "It was for Episode 8, which wasn't completely written yet. The director of that episode, Seith Mann, wasn't available yet, so I shot it," says Glatter.

For what purpose? "There was early talk of Saul going down to Venezuela and finding Brody and executing him," Alex Gansa reveals. "We liked the idea that he went down there, found this man, and, for the sake of the country, killed him. But that was a marker in the distance at this point. We didn't know how we were going to use it, and we thought it was worth shooting while we were down there."

OPPOSITE TOP: Dr. Graham tends to Brody's wounds, with the help of young Paco. El Niño's daughter, Esme, looks on.

OPPOSITE BOTTOM: Production designer John Kretschmer and director Clark Johnson share notes during production scout for "Tower of David."

TOP: The unfinished Ponce de Leon building in San Juan, Puerto Rico, which would stand in for the real Tower of David in Caracas, Venezuela.

BOTTOM: Producer Michael Klick surveys the interior of the structure, during a scouting trip in May, a month before filming at the location.

MAJID JAVADI

MAJID JAVADI, THE DEPUTY CHIEF, Intelligence Directorate for the Iranian Revolutionary Guard Corps who ordered the attack on Langley, is a different kind of terrorist threat. "We didn't want just a simple, two-dimensional man who ordered the bombing," says showrunner Alex Gansa. "It was our job to flesh out a living, breathing person who not only Carrie and Saul respond to, but the audience does, as well."

"I never want to do a role as a terrorist, just for the sake of being a terrorist," says Shaun Toub (pronounced "toob"), the Iranian-born actor who portrays Javadi. "I need to have a backstory, to know why he is what he is. And on *Homeland*, I knew they would let me play around with him a little bit," something he and writer Patrick Harbinson pursued in "The Yoga Play," Episode 5, when the audience begins to get to know the character.

"Javadi is somebody that is going to switch allegiances, if that serves his purposes," says Gansa. "He's a survivor, he's not a fanatic." Toub agrees. "He is extremely smart. He's always

thinking. The wheels are always turning. Even when Carrie turns the tables on him, you can see he's already thinking of his next move."

He and Saul have a long history, one that has far-reaching effects on Saul's regime-change plan. "In pre-revolution Iran, in 1979, they were buddies, would hang out with their wives, have dinner," Toub explains. "Javadi was Saul's counterpart in SAVAK, the Iranian intelligence agency." But when the Revolution took place, Javadi turned his back on his friend, assassinating four assets he promised to help Saul get out of the country. "He used them as pawns, to show the new regime that he wanted to be part of them. He had to make a decision about what was going to happen to himself and think about his future. That's all he cares about."

While developing his character, Toub took an interesting approach, again, to avoid the basic, two-dimensional bad man. "He's a tough guy, but he's also charming. You see that in the way he interacts with Carrie, at times a little flirtatious, even a little caring toward her," the actor explains. "I wanted the audience to like him in certain moments. And I wanted them to be surprised that they like him."

Javadi rarely loses his cool, because, as Toub

notes, "He's a professional." He is also fastidious and tidy, an interesting aspect to a brutally vicious killer. "You see it in the way he dresses. He's not a fashionista, but he tries to dress as well as possible, without bringing too much attention to himself." Educated in the United States (thus speaking English with only the slightest hint of an accent), Javadi has missed the finer things in American life, like the hamburger he eats while observing his ex-wife's house. But the slightest drop of ketchup on his tie can ruin his day.

Javadi is the master manipulator, easily playing Saul and Carrie against each other by revealing conflicting information to each about Brody's involvement in the bombing. "He's always playing everybody against everyone," Toub relates. "He tells Saul he doesn't really know who the bomber is, but that it's not Brody. And then he tells Carrie, 'Oh, you won't believe what he asked me.' He didn't really need to tell her that. But he's always playing that chess game. It's interesting for him; he likes to disturb people. He's always thinking of how he can play one against the other."

Though forced into the position of helping the CIA, Javadi is not really against the regime-change idea. "It's not a horrible plan," Toub explains. "He thinks, 'For now, I'll be the star, I'll be the man. I'll have all the power. I'll go set up my next move and see how I'm gonna get out

TOP: The old days: a clever prop photo Saul uses to remind Javadi of days gone by, of the Berensons and Javadis enjoying a night out at a French restaurant in Tehran in 1979. The prop was made from '70s-era photographs supplied by the actors. Left to right: Mandy Patinkin (Saul), Sarita Choudhury (Mira), Mary Apick (Fariba Javadi), and Majid Javadi (Shaun Toub).

BOTTOM: Old pals: Another prop photo showing Javadi (left) and Saul (right) in their younger days, created in the same way.

SAUL GETS GOOSED

IN "THE YOGA PLAY," SAUL IS INVITED to go hunting with Senator Lockhart, where Saul is expecting it will be announced that he will be the new CIA Director. But, once there Lockhart reveals to him that he, not Saul, is being nominated for the directorship.

"It's delightful to have the upper hand over your opponent," says actor Tracy Letts. "Saul has attempted to make Lockhart look incompetent in front of his committee. So Lockhart enjoys this a great deal."

The idea came about when one of the writers noted that Tracy Letts happened to look quite a bit like former Vice President Dick Cheney, who famously shot his lawyer on such a hunt. So even though it was summertime, when there were no geese available to shoot, a hunt was arranged.

Production designer John Kretschmer and producer Michael Klick drove throughout North Carolina searching for an appropriate location. "It had to be a Senate-quality hunting lodge," Kretschmer describes. The team eventually settled on one in Waxhaw, whose wealthy owner had more than 500 trophy mounts filling the structure. "We were all set to shoot there, and then, at the last minute, the owner decided *Homeland* subject matter wasn't appropriate for him." Another lodge, known as The Fork, in Norwood, became available. "This owner was fine. He was happy to have us."

The actual duck blind was built at another location, Cowan's Ford Wildlife Refuge, located at the end of Neck Road, near where, the previous year, Brody had been kidnapped via helicopter.

After a fifteen-minute gun-safety lesson, Patinkin and Letts filmed their scene, alternating dialogue with goose hunting. The goose was one stuffed for the production by a local taxidermist and launched from a catapult built by the grip department. "Lucy" (you get it? Lucy Goosey . . .) was then retrieved by a Labrador named Rio. "Lucy made it through seven takes," recalls prop master Gillian Albinski. "We were afraid a wing was gonna come off."

A BLOODY MESS

WHEN JAVADI TURNED HIS BACK ON Saul at the time of the Iranian Revolution, murdering four of his assets, Saul retaliated by helping Javadi's wife, Fariba, immigrate to the US. The act was one for which Javadi would never forgive neither Saul nor his wife. "Javadi always said, 'One day, I'm going to settle the score with him,'" actor Shaun Toub states.

Though it was not in Javadi's plan to kill Fariba at the time we see him sitting in his car outside her house in Maryland, later when he finds himself forced to cooperate with the CIA, he decides the time has come to take his revenge. "He knows he's caught, he has nowhere to go. He has to play this game. But he wants to make life a living hell for Saul. And the only card he has to play is Fariba," Toub says.

The writers decided that Javadi needed to commit the murder in an exceptional way. "We wanted Javadi to do something brutal and unforgettable," Alex Gansa explains. While he simply shoots his daughter-in-law point blank in the

head with a gun, Javadi decides to make Fariba's death much more terrifying—and messy—opting instead to smash a bottle of Iranian wine and jam the broken glass into her neck until she bleeds to death. "He knew that that style of killing would be very messy for the CIA to clean up and would be a headache for Saul," Toub says.

At first, Toub wasn't altogether sure about portraying such an act of brutality. "I was uncomfortable with it," he admits. "I kept asking Alex, 'Tell me why he's so brutal?' It was only my second episode, and I was still trying to figure out the character. I wanted to make sure there was a reason for it."

The scene was shot at a house in Charlotte, not too far from the Brody house. "Thankfully, the owners of the house were big fans of the show, and were very welcoming," says production designer John Kretschmer. "Which was nice, because we had to commit a fairly gruesome murder in their home." To protect the house from the spraying movie blood, the art department put up false walls over the real walls, as well as their own flooring.

Prop master Gillian Albinski was keen to assure the blood spatter looked the way it would during a real such crime. "I actually talked to the medical examiner about how that would look and how the investigating team would come into the space and do their work," she says.

Though the on-set makeup "gag" by KNB EFX was fairly elaborate (with ample blood pumped from the neck of actress Mary Apick

by props specialist Kelly Rubottom), and was photographed in detail. Director Lesli Linka Glatter later decided, during editing, to show very little of the act itself onscreen. "We shot all that. But it's actually more horrifying to play on Javadi as he's doing it," she explains. "There was a film where Bob Hoskins kills a guy with a beer bottle, and I remembered it being horrifying. But when you look at it, you actually see very little." Adds Gansa, "It's subjective. How much blood do you want to see, how gruesome can it be without being too gruesome? We want to convey the brutality, but not be gratuitous."

Carrie and Quinn arrive at the house moments too late, just as Javadi is completing the act. They quickly lead him away, but Quinn is unknowingly picked up by a security camera. With police searching for this unknown figure, Quinn and Saul decide that he will return to the house to answer detectives' questions. The detective, in this case, is none other than *Homeland* director Clark Johnson, himself a veteran television actor.

The part was written specifically for Johnson by Chip Johannessen, to settle his own score of sorts. "When we were in Puerto Rico shooting 'Tower of David,' Clark and I had some 'creative discussion' about something and ended up yelling at each other in the streets," he laughs. "I love that guy, so I just wanted to do something to make up for that." Johnson enjoyed the opportunity, even if it meant playing yet another homicide detective, he says. "I've done that for seven seasons on *Homicide*. But because it's this show, and because it was such a cool, little part Chip wrote, and because they're my buddies, it was just fun to do. I enjoyed it."

TOP: Shaun Toub is photographed atop actress Mary Apick, jabbing a prop bottle into her neck.

MIDDLE: Double murder: The results of Javadi's retribution, his dead ex-wife, Fariba (Mary Apick) and daughter-in-law, Susan Roberts (Emily Donahoe). The scene was filmed in a real house, for which false walls and flooring were constructed to protect the property from spraying movie blood.

BOTTOM: *Actor* (not director this time) Clark Johnson takes direction from director Carl Franklin in Episode 7, "Gerontion."

CARRIE ALMOST GETS HER MAN

CARRIE MAY NOT HAVE SEEN BRODY since she dropped him off at the Canadian border after the Langley bombing, but proving his innocence has never been far from her mind. In "a red wheel barrow," she all but gets herself killed, trying to stop Franklin, Leland Bennett's right-hand man, from murdering the now-identified Langley bomber.

"She suddenly has a piece of ammunition, the guy who actually moved the car, in her sights," says Alex Gansa, who cowrote the episode with James Yoshimura. "She finally has the ability to exonerate Brody once and for all." Her emotions build through the episode, until they take over her entire being, he says. "She can't help but get out of the car and try and stop Franklin from killing this person that means everything to her," quickly prompting an order by Dar Adal for Quinn to shoot her—to stop her in her tracks before she ruins the operation. Franklin quietly approaches the room of the bomber, Monroe (Aaron Serotsky), at the Fairview Motel (actually the City Center Inn, downtown on Tryon Street), and shoots him in the head. It is then his job to get rid of the body, so that Monroe can never be identified.

We see Franklin drag the body to the bathtub, pull out two jugs of acid and pour them over the body, which is out of frame, so that only the resulting smoke is visible. "He was originally going to pour the acid over his face, and we were going to do a face melt effect," says prop master Gillian Albinski. "But that got dropped before we got before the cameras."

Another effect that was planned, which did end up getting photographed, was one in which Franklin snipped off Monroe's fingertips with a pair of gardening shears, in order to remove any fingerprints, of course. To create the effect, a plaster cast was made of actor Serotsky's arm, and detailed photographs taken, from which several color-matched duplicates of his arm and hand were made from foam latex. "They even put in the hairs," says Albinski. "It was pretty amazing."

The shot, unfortunately, remains on the cutting room floor.

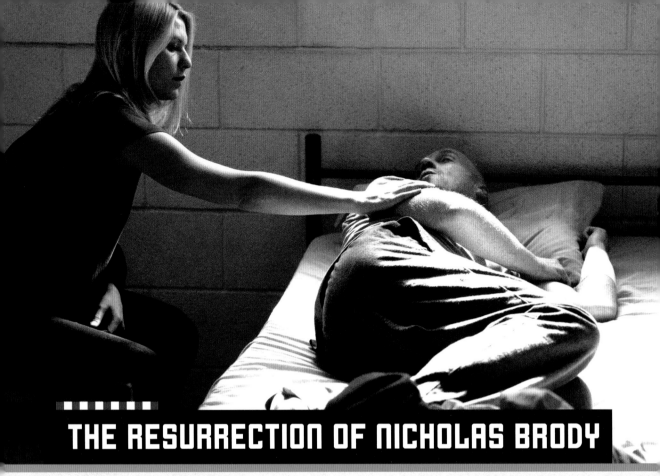

THE RESURRECTION OF NICHOLAS BRODY

ONCE THE WRITERS KNEW THEY WANTED to build their story around a regime change, and knew Javadi would be involved, the question became how to work Brody into the puzzle.

For the moment, Brody was "embracing the poppy," addicted to heroin in the Tower of David down in Caracas. That situation gave the writers a chance to explore something new— a season of *Homeland* that was *not* Brody/Carrie-centric. "Once Brody became a junkie, we knew that he was going to be out of commission," informs showrunner Alex Gansa. "That gave us the opportunity to have a run of episodes without him, kind of as a test case, to see if the show could function, could thrive, without Brody on screen."

The show, it turns out, was just as compelling. "We learned first and foremost that the relationship between Carrie and Saul is a powerful one, and a complex one. That's where the show gravitates to without Brody. The relationship between mentor and protégé."

It also gave Damian Lewis a chance to fit in some side work. His absence from Episodes 4 through 8 (from about mid-June to the second week in September) allowed the actor to go to Scotland to film *The Silent Storm* for director Corinna McFarlane. "Once it was clear that I was going to have this gap, my friends at *Homeland* were very generous. They helped to make that work," Lewis notes.

The question remained, how to involve Brody? And how to get him out of the Tower of David? Around the time "Tower of David" was being written, Patrick Harbinson, Chip Johannessen's writing partner from *24*, arrived to join the writing team. "We had a lot of ideas, and we weren't quite sure how to lay them out," Johannessen recalls. "We were committed to the idea of the Javadi character, and to having his boss be the ultimate target. But then Patrick really helped with working the Brody assassination operation into play."

Brody could get out of the Tower of David in one of two ways. "It seemed to us that he could either be sprung by al-Qaeda or Hezbollah operatives, or the CIA could find him," Gansa explains. Having an operation in which to involve him tilted the scales toward the latter solution. "Saul had always had a two-part operation in mind, the second of which, sending Brody back in, he had never told Carrie about. So he had to twist some arms and piece together who might have been involved in Carrie's underground railroad, and eventually figured out where Brody was, even if Carrie didn't know herself."

That, of course, put an end to the "alternate use" of the footage shot in June of Saul in the Tower of David. Brody would be brought back to life, for the moment.

In the ninth episode, "One Last Thing" (originally titled "Horse and Wagon," the name of the motel where Brody later meets Dana), Saul retrieves Brody and takes him to a Special Ops base, where two Navy SEALs and two Marines walk him through his withdrawal from heroin, and then begin the process of rehabilitating him back to his old Marine self.

While the interiors for the scenes of Brody's withdrawal and rehabilitation were filmed on sets at the *Homeland* stages, the exteriors (running, training, etc.) were shot at the Gastonia Police training base in Gastonia, North Carolina. "When you're doing military and government, you don't make it up. It really needs to be done properly," says production designer John Kretschmer. Adds producer Michael Klick, "The base had it all, with trails, an obstacle course, and shooting ranges. And what it didn't have, we adjusted the story to match what was there."

Brody endures hellish withdrawal symptoms due to a controversial drug Saul orders used, called ibogaine, in order to speed up the process (and get the operation started before Lockhart has a chance to stop it). "We were doing research about what it was like to withdraw from heroin, and if there was any way to speed it up, and we found ibogaine," explains Gansa.

Brody goes through everything from intense vomiting (created by the props department using the usual combination of mushroom soup, applesauce, and oatmeal, though the scenes were left unused), hallucinations, and even compulsive masturbation (also cut). "We must have spent three or four days trying to figure out the nature of what his hallucinations would be," Gansa says. The team eventually settled on having Brody flash back to singing a song with Tom Walker. Brody also flashes back to his own suicide attempt (a scene that featured a reprise for actor Navid Negahban), which was stopped by Abu Nazir himself—an act Brody repeats in real time, using a broken chair leg in his barracks room, and which is almost successful.

BELOW RIGHT: "One Last Thing" writer Barbara Hall and director Jeffrey Reiner take a break during filming.

Through his work with the Special Ops team, Brody eventually gets back on his feet. "It was a way to reach back and reconnect him with that person that he once was, and that was Saul's goal," says Gansa, adding, "We had a whole montage of him running and shooting, etc. And when the editors first cut it together, they put the *Rocky* score over it," he laughs.

Inspired by the camaraderie of his Special Ops buddies, Brody physically comes back, but he still has no desire to move forward. So Saul is forced to bring in the "big guns," a.k.a. Carrie, whom he visits in the hospital where she is recovering from the gunshot wound she suffered in the previous episode. "There's a lot of ground that has to be healed there," says director Lesli Linka Glatter. She shot the scenes for director Jeffrey Reiner, who had suffered a loss in his family and was unable to complete the episode. "It was an amazing scene to walk into and shoot, because it was such a turning point scene."

Glatter also shot Episode 9's long-awaited reunion of Brody and Carrie in the barracks room, the first time the two are seen together in Season 3. "The way Lesli shot it is really beautiful," says Gansa. "We linger there for almost forty-five seconds before Brody turns to face her."

Brody finally sees that participating in, and completing, the mission is a way to attain a kind of redemption, which is particularly important to him in regard to his relationship with his daughter. He requests one favor from Carrie:

that she takes Brody to see Dana one last time. "That scene was an expression of all the emotions Dana's been feeling toward her father, and toward Carrie," notes says Morgan Saylor. "I think she probably had thought about what she would say a million times, if this ever happened. I think she said the right things."

While incredibly heartbreaking for the audience to watch, Dana's reaction to Brody has the right effect on him, notes Johannessen. "It actually galvanizes him to do this mission, to redeem himself."

ABOVE: The chair leg with which Brody stabs his arm (this one thankfully made of rubber) while in an hallucinogenic haze.

BELOW: Brody and the Special Ops team help bring the fallen Marine back to life, in scene filmed at the Gastonia Police training base in North Carolina.

ACTION AT THE BORDER

SEASON 3's TENTH EPISODE, "Good Night," brings Brody across the border. He's gone full circle from isolated junkie in Caracas back to full-fledged Marine. "It was our chance to make a little war movie," notes showrunner Alex Gansa. The episode was directed by Keith Gordon, whose first feature film in 1992 was a World War II indie war film, *A Midnight Clear.*

The script was cowritten by Alex Cary and staff writer Charlotte Stoudt, who had previously been working with the writing team and now got her chance to apply her skills in earnest. Cary's contributions, once again, took advantage of his own experiences, not only with military operations, but also with relationships between soldiers. This is evident in the affectionate banter between Brody and his Special Ops colleagues: Azizi, Turani, Modarres, and Baraz.

While the setting certainly looks authentic, the battlefield scenes were actually filmed at the Bessemer City Quarry, located about forty-five minutes outside of Charlotte. "When I first read the script, I thought, 'Guys, we're in Charlotte, North Carolina, which is green and lush in the summer. There is no Iraqi/Irani border here,'" recalls director Lesli Linka Glatter. "But our amazing location scout, Kathy Berry, suggested this closed-down quarry she had seen on Google Maps and had an instinct that it might work for us. And it was amazing looking."

As production designer John Kretschmer describes, "Beside the quarry pit, there's a

A day at the quarry: The Special Ops cast pose with director Lesli Linka Glatter and writer Alex Cary on September 30, the first day of filming at the Bessemer City Quarry. Left to right: Walid Amini, Damian Lewis, Donnie Keshawarz, Glatter, Jaylen Moore, Jared Ward, Alex Cary.

man-made mountain of spoil rock, which was quite massive. Plenty of rock and weeds, so it was perfect." At least as far as the camera sees, notes producer Michael Klick. "Director of photography David Klein did a masterful job shooting this at night. Night shooting hides a lot, particularly the fact that our 'Iraq' was surrounded by a lush green forest! You just don't point your lights that direction."

TOP: Dummies for Brody and Azizi get ready to take the hit in the IED truck explosion.

BOTTOM: Explosion aftermath: The pickup truck, post-IED.

OPPOSITE: There's always time to check on things at home: Claire Danes on Rue Belgrade, the street on which the home of Nassrin, Abu Nazir's widow, could be found.

The cast and crew were not alone at the quarry. "There were plenty of snakes and coyotes out there, even some wild goats," says stunt coordinator Cal Johnson.

Johnson and his stunt team's skills were put to the test. "Good Night" was the most stunt-heavy episode of the entire series. One major scene involved blowing up Brody's and Azizi's pickup truck, when it strikes an IED. Says Johnson, "We scouted with the director and the effects guys, Larry and Ray Bivins, and figured out where we wanted the explosion to happen and how we wanted the truck to explode." The truck literally folded in half from the force of the explosion. "That surprised everybody. We thought it was going to just turn over and land on its side, but it shot it straight up in the air and folded it in half, which actually looked better onscreen," Johnson says. "I was originally going to drive the truck into the explosion, but we ended up just towing it in with a cable a few inches off the ground. It came out great."

Another complex stunt involved the "farm-house" in which Brody hides after dashing away from the others, which is then hit by a mortar. The house was a set Kretschmer built at the quarry, and Damian Lewis did his own stunt work, as he did for much of the episode. "Damian actually wanted to try to do most the stuff there, and he did, though we had a double for him when needed," Johnson relates.

Though, prior to the mission, Brody managed his way through his training, he is by no means the Marine he once was. Several times he finds himself frightened enough to abandon the mission, and his fear prompts Azizi to chide him with another memorable piece of Alex Cary military banter: "It's a little late for your vagina to be chiming in."

"Remember, this is the place where Brody was captured, and where he endured all of that suffering," Gansa explains. "So it was inevitable that being back there was going to bring some of that old stuff up, and it indeed does. The terror of reliving those moments cannot have been easy for Brody. But somehow he reaches down and finds some strength, and carries on."

FILMING IN MOROCCO

THE FINAL TWO EPISODES OF THE season, depicting Brody and Carrie in Iran, were intended to be filmed in Israel using Gideon Raff's *Hatufim* crew, as the series' previous Middle East locations had been shot, but that never happened. As the time approached to prep for the two episodes, in late August/early September, the Syrian uprising reached a dangerous level, and there was concern about security in Israel, so Fox decided it would be safer to find another location.

At the time, the studio was filming the pilot for Raff's and Howard Gordon's new series, *Tyrant*, in Marrakesh, Morocco, so Fox suggested *Homeland* shoot in Morocco as well. Producer Michael Klick arrived in Morocco on September 25, as *Tyrant* was wrapping up and ten days later moved the *Tyrant* production team to the coastal city of Rabat, 175 miles to the north, to film the final episodes of *Homeland*. The crew included members from eight different countries, including France, Italy, and Hungary,

as well as thirty-five crewmembers that flew in from Charlotte, accompanied by large amounts of equipment. The crew would remain in Rabat from October 22 through November 6, working six-day weeks.

Producer Michael Klick and Episode 11 director Dan Minahan scoured the region for locations. The production office was set up in the Le Dawliz Hotel, across the Bou Regreg River from Rabat in Sale (pronounced SAH-lay). "The hotel had a bunch of nightclubs and restaurants which weren't in use, so those became our offices," Klick explains. Sale, incidentally, was the location where Ridley Scott's 2001 hit *Black Hawk Down* was photographed. "Some of our guys worked on that and showed us the locations, which was pretty interesting."

A short drive across the river in Rabat was the beautiful Sofitel Rabat Jardin des Roses hotel, where a good number of Charlotte crew and cast stayed. The Sofitel appeared in *Homeland* as the Grand Hotel, where Carrie stays when she comes to coordinate with Brody and where she is eventually intercepted by Javadi's men. A part of the hotel was also used for the scene where Damian Lewis is filmed publicly denouncing the United States on Iranian television.

Morocco's Ministry of Finance building was used as the Iranian Revolutionary Guard Corps (IRGC) office, where Brody comes to murder Akbari. Those scenes were filmed over the weekends of October 26 and November 2. Minahan and director Lesli Linka Glatter, who directed the finale, took turns completing their required scenes. "The whole government complex is across the street from the king's palace," Klick explains. So how did *Homeland* get permission to use important government buildings for an American TV show, even to depict a murder in one of the episodes? "The way business is handled there, everything is dependent on who you know, and our locations folks apparently knew the right people. And they were really wonderful to us."

The compound where Brody is kept upon arriving from Iraq was actually the Lycée Hassan II, a French school in the center of Rabat. The crew filmed on the weekend, because classes took place there during the week.

Carrie and Brody make an escape to a safe house, where they await rescue, though are ultimately captured by Javadi's men. The farmhouse used as the safe house was located forty-five minutes to the south of Rabat, in the town of Aïn El Aouda. "We spent quite a lot of time looking for a location like the one Alex Gansa had in mind, which was a more desert-y location than the one we actually used," Klick describes.

The exterior of the mosque, in which Carrie warns Brody that he is a target, is actually that of an older palace, the Palais Tazi, located adjacent to Morocco's Parliament building. It was a site used in *Tyrant*. Klick says, "The building has fallen on hard times, but it's still a beautiful location. Incredible texture, and, as I like to say: 'not California.'" A lot next to the Palais was used as the site for the Brody hanging.

Director Lesli Linka Glatter explains a scene to Claire Danes and Alex Gansa in the anteroom of a palace—actually the Palais Raissouni in Rabat. In the scene, Carrie calls Saul one last time in a vain attempt to save Brody from execution.

WILL HE OR WON'T HE?

BY EPISODE 11, "BIG MAN IN TEHRAN," Brody appears to be back on track to complete his mission, and maybe, just maybe, there's a chance for his safe return. But would he?

Carrie arrives in Iran and arranges for Brody to receive a syringe filled with cyanide with which to kill Akbari. But Brody is thrown off when Akbari takes him to see Abu Nazir's widow, Nassrin (played by Naz Deravian), to vet Brody and make certain his intentions are true. Upon leaving her house, Brody suddenly finds himself a hero in the eyes of the Iranian public, and he considers staying in Iran for good.

"He's beginning to doubt if he is ever going to find peace anywhere and be able to have any kind of life," explains showrunner Alex Gansa. "He says it to Carrie outside the mosque, 'Go where? Do what? There's no life for me anywhere. I'm not going back, I can't go on the run. This is a place where I could actually live.' I think the idea has some validity, and he's weighing it in his mind."

Brody tosses the syringe (actually a complex and expensive prop brought from Charlotte for just such a purpose) and seems to give up the idea of killing Akbari. But he arranges to meet with Akbari, apparently to spill the beans on Javadi, or so Javadi believes. "Brody has gone to Nazir's wife and told her, 'Tell Akbari that I want to see him about Javadi,'" actor Shaun Toub says. "Javadi happens to see Brody coming into the Ministry, going to Akbari's office. There's no other reason for him to be there. So Javadi puts two and two together and realizes, 'Holy shit, he's going to give me away.' All the plans are falling apart.'"

Brody does go in to see Akbari, and he actually does tell him about Javadi's role with the CIA. But what makes him go through with the assassination? "Brody's a completely unpredictable character," says Gansa. "I think he realizes that the end is near, and that he has to go out with some kind of heroic action. And I think sitting in that office with Akbari is when he makes the decision."

The audience is left with a cliffhanger, reminiscent of their experiences watching *24*. How will Brody get out of this one? "Episodes 11 and 12 were meant to be one big episode, in a sense," Gansa explains. "If you notice, Episode 12 picked right up when it aired—we had no main titles or recap. We went right into the story. Anybody who was watching the finale had watched Episode 11."

Brody escapes, with the help of Carrie (who, as usual, has defied orders to leave the country), and after informing Saul that Brody indeed completed the mission, the couple drives to a safe house to await their rescue. In a scene written by Meredith Stiehm, who had returned to cowrite the finale (having left to create *The Bridge* for FX), Brody and Carrie discuss a possible future. "We had to give the audience a sense that there was a chance that they could possibly get out of there and begin a new life," says Gansa, "that those helicopters are actually coming." The two even appear to have what amounts to a domestic argument of sorts. "It wasn't a romantic scene; they're arguing, almost like husband and wife. We were hoping to convince the audience that, 'Oh, my God, they're talking about actually being together after this.'"

But Brody is still in despair, believing he has no future. "Carrie feels that he's finally redeemed himself, and has finally proven to everybody that he is actually the man she always thought he was," Gansa says. "And the only way to get him out of this funk is to tell him the truth, that she's carrying his child," a seed that

Gansa says had been planted in Episode 6, "Still Positive," for this very purpose.

"He's in existential despair," notes Lesli Linka Glatter. "And when Carrie tells him that she's pregnant, that's a game changer. The only thing that makes any sense for him is that there's some sort of new life starting."

"We knew these were going to be Brody and Carrie's last moments together," says Alex Gansa, "so their conversation had to leave the audience with something to think about."

ABOVE LEFT: Damian Lewis takes a breather in the "green room" at Morocco's Ministry of Finance, the building used for the IRGC. Perhaps he is contemplating whether Brody will indeed go through with the assassination.

ABOVE LEFT: The cyanide syringe props, intended for killing Akbari.

BELOW: Prop master Gillian Albinski displays a prop visa for 33-year-old Swiss national, Madeleine Bezieux—a.k.a. Carrie Mathison.

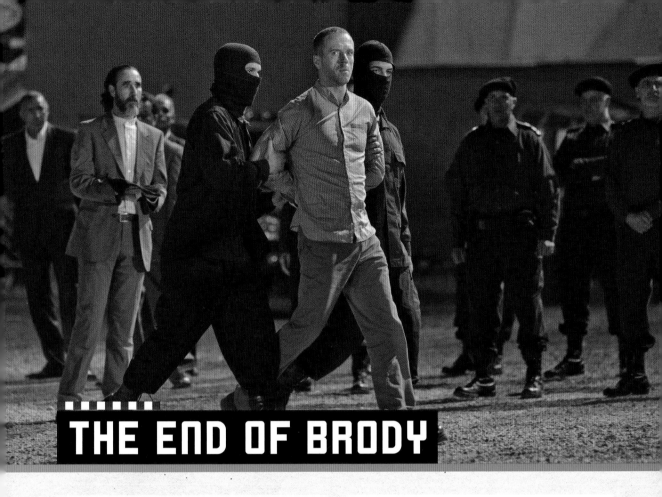

THE END OF BRODY

WHILE CARRIE AND BRODY await their extraction, Javadi convinces Dar Adal and Lockhart—who in turn convince the President—that Brody cannot return. "It's better for the operation, it's better for Javadi's ascent to a position of power, and ultimately," says showrunner Alex Gansa, "it's better in Saul's eyes for Carrie, even though he won't admit it."

The CIA would have no way of explaining that Brody was a CIA asset who was sent to Iran to kill Akbari. "If that information ever comes out, Javadi will never ascend to the position, and the mission will have been a failure. So Brody's existence is a problem for everyone. He has to be sacrificed to the Iranians."

While Carrie cannot fathom the possibility of his execution, Brody seems to have come to terms with his own end. For his part, the road has never been easy. "The moment he went to war to fight for his country was the moment that everything changed," says actor Damian Lewis. "Within six months of being deployed,

he'd been captured and was being tortured. And now, having been in exile, isolated from his family, exhausted from being on the run, I think he looks back on what's happened to him over the last nine years. He has an opportunity to look at the bigger picture."

"Brody's post-Iraq life has been an ugly existence," says Gansa. "Look what's happened to his family, what's happened to him. The death that surrounds him is weighing on his soul in a way that is untenable for him." Notes Lewis, "He's a man who is succumbing to battle fatigue. That battle that has been his life."

The methodology for doing away with Brody took some discussion among the writers. "Originally, we had Carrie and Brody making this miraculous escape, and then they played out a coda where it looked like they would be together, and then he was taken out," recalls writer Chip Johannessen. "But it became clear that was the wrong story. So we made it that he would get caught and be hanged."

Such hangings are not unusual in Iran, says director Lesli Linka Glatter. "I did a lot of research on the Internet, and we based it on what you see if you search. These things are very matter of fact. They just put a big construction crane off to the side of the road, and people come and watch. It's horrible."

To execute the hanging stunt, producer Michael Klick found a rig used for previous movie hangings. "It's a kind of a body harness that includes a set of stirrups," he explains. "You're not really hanging from your thighs, like a mountaineering rig would have. Part of the weight's taken by your feet." The rig can make it difficult for the actor to appear to be hanging naturally, because when so much weight is placed on the feet, the actor's legs tend to spread, as was the case with Lewis, who did the stunt himself.

A test of the rig was performed in the parking lot of the Le Dawliz Hotel, on October 19, two and a half weeks before the shoot, with Italian stunt-actor Jérémie Vigot successfully and safely suspended.

The hanging itself, Scene B1243, was performed and photographed on the night of Wednesday, November 6, in a lot near the Palais Tazi, with three cameras rolling. A total of 400 extras were hired, all of whom had to sign a waiver agreeing to keep their participation, and what they were watching, a secret, including not using cell phones or taking any pictures. Even the day's call sheets made no mention of a "Brody hangs 'till dead" scene, in case one slipped loose. "Had we been able to shoot in Israel, as we had originally planned," says Gansa, "we could never have hanged Brody from a noose in a square and kept it a secret. But somehow in Morocco, word just didn't get out."

That doesn't mean that somebody didn't try. "The first time the crane lifted Damian up to be hung, all of a sudden, he started pointing to somebody in the crowd," Gansa recalls.

THIRD: One for posterity: Damian Lewis takes a photo on his last day of filming *Homeland*.

BOTTOM: Director Lesli Linka Glatter discusses the scene setup with Alex Gansa and Claire Danes.

> *"To see someone you care about hanging by the neck, even though it's fake, and he's fine, it was still incredibly emotional. Everyone was crying."*
>
> — LESLI LINKA GLATTER, Director

"And there was a woman, in a black chador, who had her cell phone out and was filming it." The phone was immediately confiscated, and the footage deleted, and the lady in the chador was escorted out of the square.

The experience of watching Nicholas Brody hang until dead, and thus end the tenure of one of television's most popular stars of late, was hard on everyone. "The first couple of times that crane raised him up into the air, you definitely felt it in your gut," Alex Gansa relates. "It was really, really moving on a number of levels to be there, not the least of which was saying good-bye to one of the stars of the show. He's someone I just have amazing affection and respect for."

The scene affected everyone. "We wrapped at dawn, so the sun was coming up," says director Lesli Linka Glatter. "And, you know, to see someone you care about hanging by the neck, even though it's fake and he's fine, it was still incredibly emotional. Everyone was crying."

By the end of the shoot, even the veteran Gansa was overcome with emotion. "I was exhausted and had to duck into a little private square to shed a few tears," he recalls. "One of the Moroccan ADs, a young woman, found me there. She came up and put her arms around me and said, 'Sir, it will all be all right.'"

As for Lewis, after completing his scenes (which were followed by reverse shots of Claire Danes, showing Carrie's reaction), says Klick, "I think he went home and took a shower, and got on a plane at noon that day and went back to London." He did, however, leave the crew with a special gift, prop master Gillian Albinski states. "He gave each of us, as a wrap gift, a T-shirt that said, 'I Am an American.'"

Italian stunt actor Jérémie Vigot tries on the Brody hanging harness in the parking lot of the Le Dawliz Hotel.

"THE STAR"

WHILE MOST TELEVISION FINALES would have ended when a lead character died, *Homeland's* season closer continues, because life goes on.

"The most interesting story would not have been about the gnashing of teeth, the spilling of tears and the accusations," says showrunner Alex Gansa. "That would have been incredibly melodramatic. What felt far more interesting to us was that Carrie gets over it. She's a career woman, and if she is going to continue to be an intelligence officer, she has to come to terms with what happened, and then take the next step."

That next step comes in the form of an offer from her new boss, Senator Lockhart, to head a field office overseas to keep track of Javadi and his operation. "She's made so many mistakes over the course of all this," says actor Tracy Letts. "But the truth is, she's a remarkable agent. She's done a lot of remarkable things, so she deserves the shot Lockhart is giving her."

"What use would it have been to quit the CIA in protest?" asks Gansa. "She's still an intelligence officer, and that's what she does, it's what she loves to do. And if she wants to continue doing it, she better goddamn well make peace with the new director."

By the way, when Carrie arrives at Lockhart's office to discuss the matter, she is first greeted by his assistant, a character identified in the script by the name Dave Weissman and played by a newcomer to acting, Jack Solomon—director Lesli Linka Glatter's assistant.

And in case you were wondering what Tracy Letts is typing on his computer as she walks in, well, Alex Gansa wondered, too. "This is a Pulitzer Prize–winning playwright," Gansa says. "I leaned onto the set and told him, 'Tracy, you know, whatever you're writing, we own!'"

Regarding motherhood, Carrie's decision about raising her baby no doubt will be revealed in Season 4. "I think for intelligence officers, and case officers in particular, that's a real conflict," says Gansa. Not to mention the fact that it's Brody's child. "There's a lot of emotion pouring through her at that time, but also a kind of stoicism and a restraint, in terms of her career."

The agency holds its annual ceremony to honor its fallen, unveiling stars that have been engraved on the wall of the entrance in their memory. "That was something Henry always wanted to put in," notes writer Chip Johannessen. "The writing on the wall had been around since the end of last year, so we thought it might be a cool way to end the season."

Production designer John Kretschmer wished, as always, to represent military matters accurately. "Geoff Grimsman, our art director, realized that the stars in the real CIA lobby were engraved, so we had a contractor actually rout ours into the stone wall we built, to appear the way they do in the CIA's lobby."

Carrie requests Lockhart provide an engraved star for Brody, but he refuses. "As Lockhart says, 'His previous actions cast a long shadow,'" says Letts. "And I think that's very true. No, he's not getting a star on the wall. Not on my watch." Not even an anonymous one, as are many of the stars, in fact. "The names are written in an accompanying book, and many

of them don't have a name because the agent was involved with covert operations," Gansa explains. "But Lockhart wouldn't even go for an anonymous one." Meet the new boss.

But Carrie is never afraid to go against the grain. Returning late at night, she takes a black marker and draws in an anonymous star for her beloved Brody, lest he be forgotten.

The episode was untitled until just prior to airing. "We were struggling with a title for a long time," Gansa notes. "The Star," a double reference to both Carrie's impromptu decoration of Brody and the loss of one of the series's leads, was perfectly apropos.

"That was the end of the Brody/Carrie novel," says Gansa. "When Brody was executed over in Morocco, Claire got emotional too, as we all did. "We had all been through so much, worked so hard, and this really felt like an ending." Lewis is proud of the work he did as Nicholas Brody. "Brody turned out to be a sensitive soul," the actor says. "He might have been a regular blue-collar working-class guy who went to war. But after two or three years of systematically being tortured, he was a changed man—irreparably. His descent into the nine circles of hell is really what we witnessed. And now it's over."

ACKNOWLEDGMENTS

The author would like to thank the following individuals for their time and gracious assistance in the making of this book: Alex Gansa, Howard Gordon, Gideon Raff, Claire Danes, Damian Lewis, Michael Cuesta, Chip Johannessen, Alex Cary, Meredith Stiehm, Michael Klick, Lesli Linka Glatter, John Kretschmer, Patti Podesta, Gillian Albinski, Clark Johnson, Guy Ferland, Jeremy Podeswa, Morena Baccarin, Morgan Saylor, David Harewood, Navid Negahban, Rupert Friend, F. Murray Abraham, Jamey Sheridan, Diego Klattenhoff, Tracy Letts, Marin Ireland, Shaun Toub, Marc Menchaca, Zulekha Robinson, Erik Dellums, Timothée Chalamet, Sam Underwood, Judy Henderson, Michael Lane, Jay Yeomans MD, Mike Leone, John Bayless, and Joshua Izzo at Fox. And all at Chronicle Books, especially Sarah Malarkey, Beth Weber, Elizabeth Yarborough, and Neil Egan. Special thanks to Ashley Brim, Jose Cabrera, Charlotte Stoudt and Katie Schafer. And to a real *Homeland* widow, Rosie Vidaurri.

Unit and gallery photography by Ronen Akerman, Frank Balthazar, Didier Baverel, Jim Bridges, Jackson Lee Davis, Patrick Ecclesine, Nadav Kander, Bob Leverone, Frank Ockenfels 3, and Kent Smith. Additional behind-the-scenes images by Gillian Albinski, Jose Cabrera, Rob Chand, Ken Collins, Lesli Linka Glatter, Art Director Geoffrey S. Grimsman, Tom Hohman, Matt Hurwitz, Michael Klick, John D. Kretschmer, Patti Podesta, Kelly Rubottom, Todd Spencer, and Meredith Stiehm. Additional credits: Page 10, *Prisoners of War*, Season 2, Keshet Broadcasting, Photographer: Ronen Akerman. Page 88, Photo by Pete Souza/The White House.

Library of Congress Cataloging-in-Publication Data

Hurwitz, Matt.
  Homeland revealed / written by Matt Hurwitz ; foreword by Alex Gansa.
    pages cm
  ISBN 978-1-4521-2840-5 (alk. paper)
  1. Homeland (Television program : 2011–) I. Title.

  PN1992.77.H615H88 2014
  791.45'72—dc23

                         2014013820

Manufactured in China

Design by Jacob Covey

10 9 8 7 6 5 4 3 2 1

Chronicle Books LLC
680 Second Street
San Francisco, California 94107
www.chroniclebooks.com